EPICURUS THE SAGE
VOLUME II

THE MANY LOVES OF ZEUS

WM MESSNER-LOEBS WRITER ◆ SAM KIETH ILLUSTRATOR
STEVE OLIFF COLOR ARTIST

— PIRANHA PRESS —

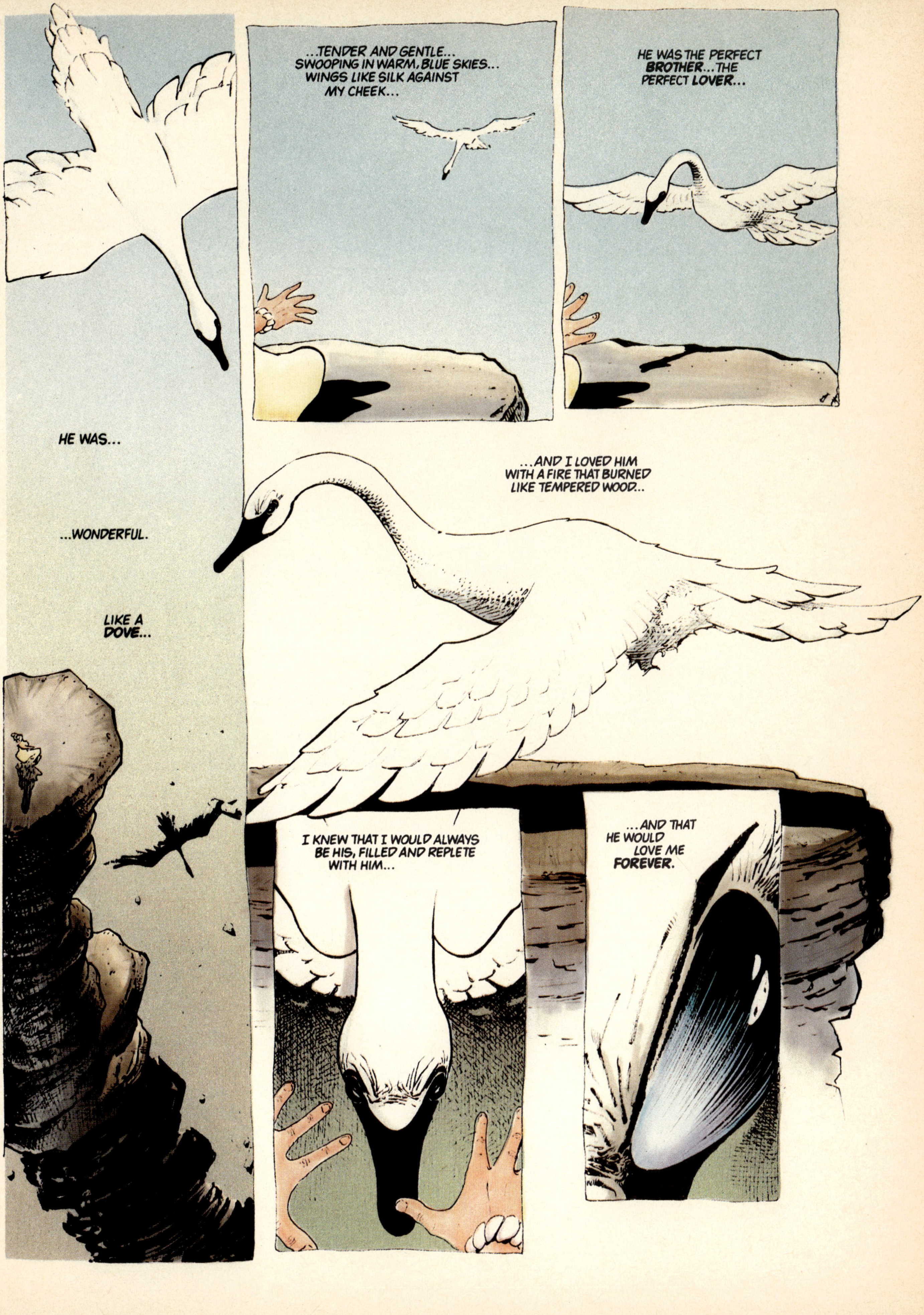
...TENDER AND GENTLE... SWOOPING IN WARM, BLUE SKIES... WINGS LIKE SILK AGAINST MY CHEEK...
HE WAS THE PERFECT **BROTHER**...THE PERFECT **LOVER**...
HE WAS...
...WONDERFUL.
LIKE A **DOVE**...
...AND I LOVED HIM WITH A FIRE THAT BURNED LIKE TEMPERED WOOD...
I KNEW THAT I WOULD ALWAYS BE HIS, FILLED AND REPLETE WITH HIM...
...AND THAT HE WOULD LOVE ME **FOREVER**.

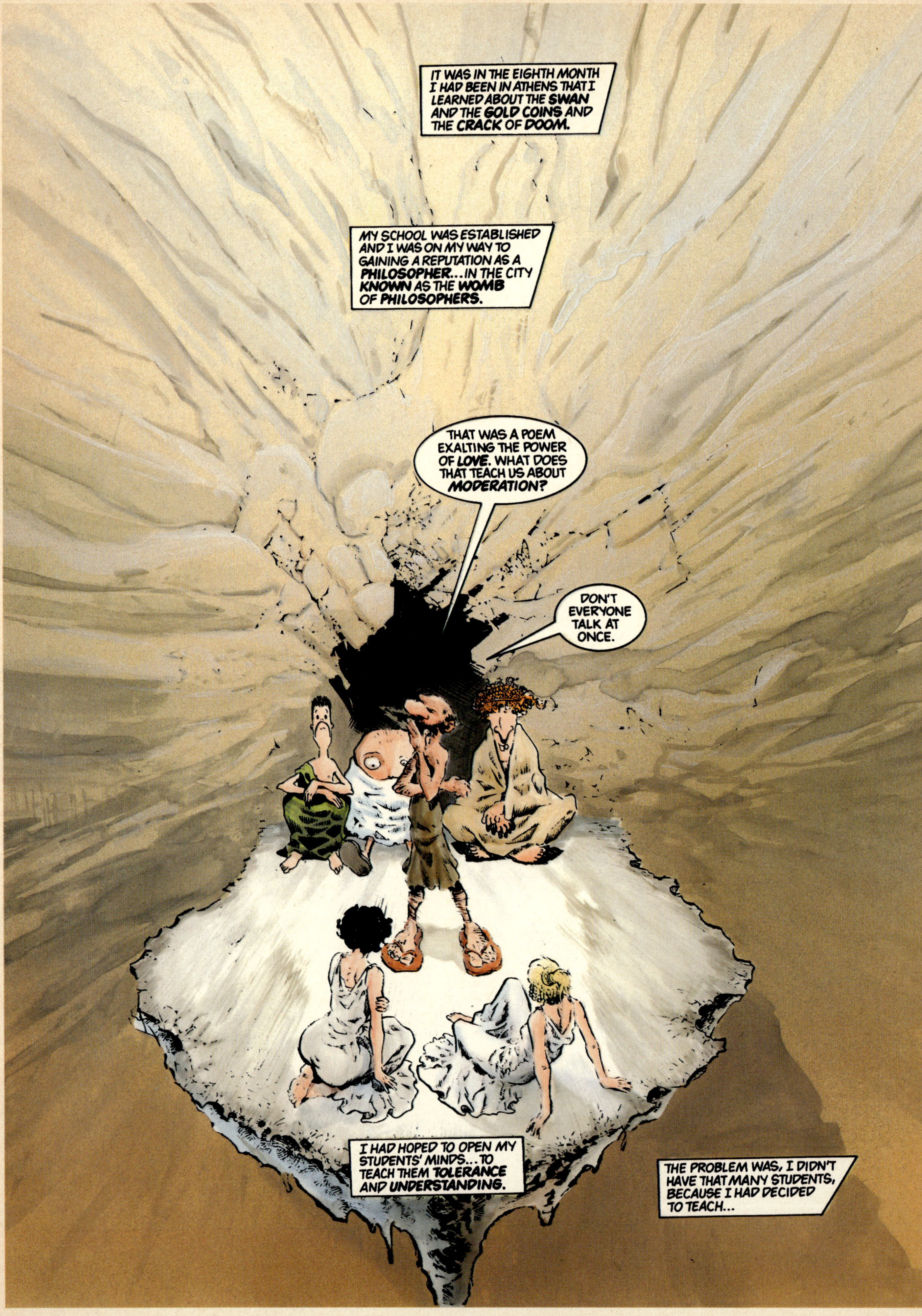

IT WAS IN THE EIGHTH MONTH I HAD BEEN IN ATHENS THAT I LEARNED ABOUT THE **SWAN** AND THE **GOLD COINS** AND THE **CRACK** OF **DOOM**.
MY SCHOOL WAS ESTABLISHED AND I WAS ON MY WAY TO GAINING A REPUTATION AS A **PHILOSOPHER**... IN THE CITY **KNOWN** AS THE **WOMB** OF **PHILOSOPHERS**.
THAT WAS A POEM EXALTING THE POWER OF **LOVE**. WHAT DOES THAT TEACH US ABOUT ***MODERATION?***
DON'T EVERYONE TALK AT ONCE.
I HAD HOPED TO OPEN MY STUDENTS' MINDS... TO TEACH THEM **TOLERANCE** AND **UNDERSTANDING**.
THE PROBLEM WAS, I DIDN'T HAVE THAT MANY STUDENTS, BECAUSE I HAD DECIDED TO TEACH...

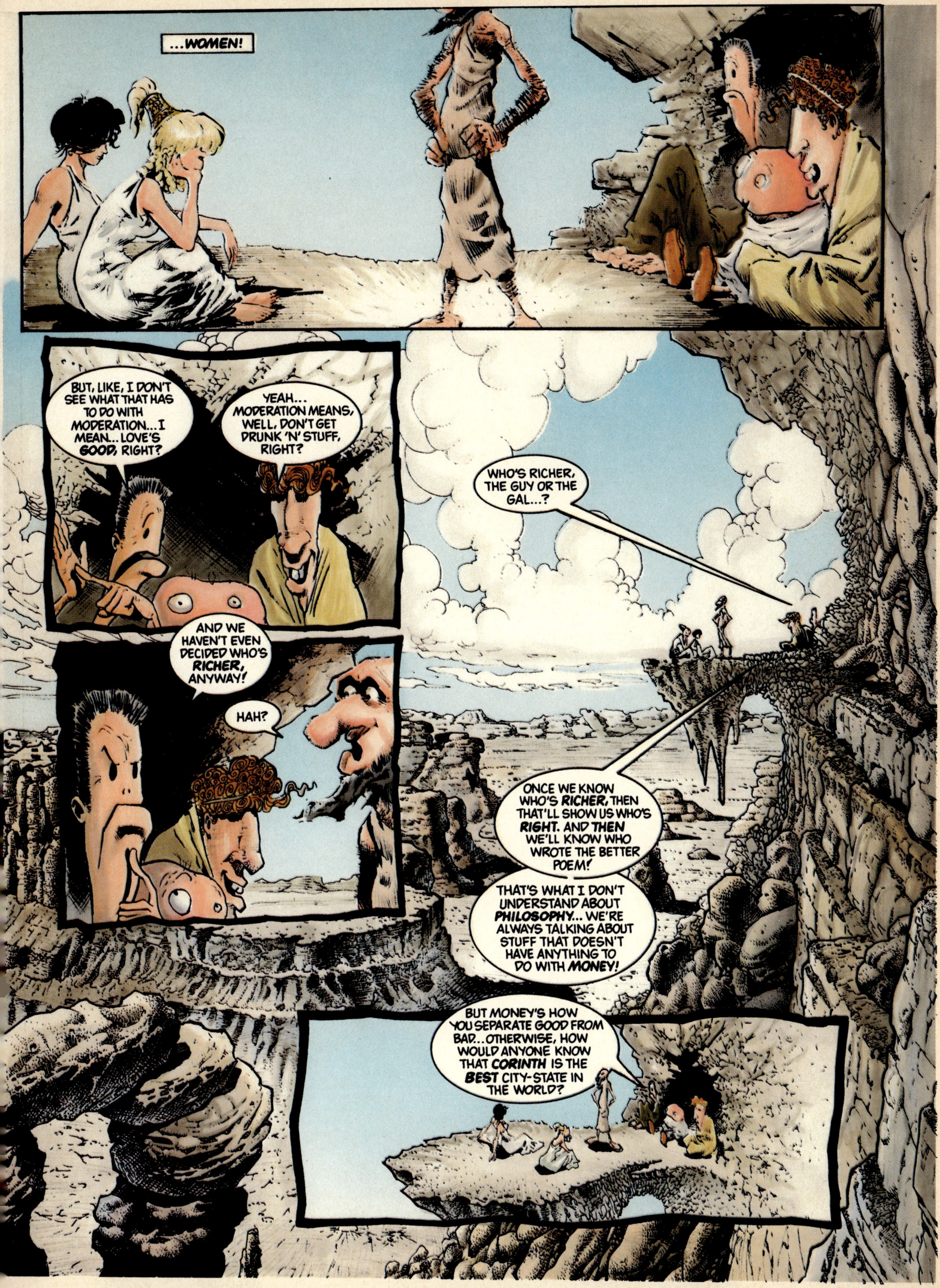
...WOMEN!
BUT, LIKE, I DON'T SEE WHAT THAT HAS TO DO WITH MODERATION... I MEAN... LOVE'S GOOD, RIGHT?
YEAH... MODERATION MEANS, WELL, DON'T GET DRUNK 'N' STUFF, RIGHT?
WHO'S RICHER, THE GUY OR THE GAL...?
AND WE HAVEN'T EVEN DECIDED WHO'S RICHER, ANYWAY!
HAH?
ONCE WE KNOW WHO'S RICHER, THEN THAT'LL SHOW US WHO'S RIGHT. AND THEN WE'LL KNOW WHO WROTE THE BETTER POEM!
THAT'S WHAT I DON'T UNDERSTAND ABOUT PHILOSOPHY... WE'RE ALWAYS TALKING ABOUT STUFF THAT DOESN'T HAVE ANYTHING TO DO WITH MONEY!
BUT MONEY'S HOW YOU SEPARATE GOOD FROM BAD... OTHERWISE, HOW WOULD ANYONE KNOW THAT CORINTH IS THE BEST CITY-STATE IN THE WORLD?

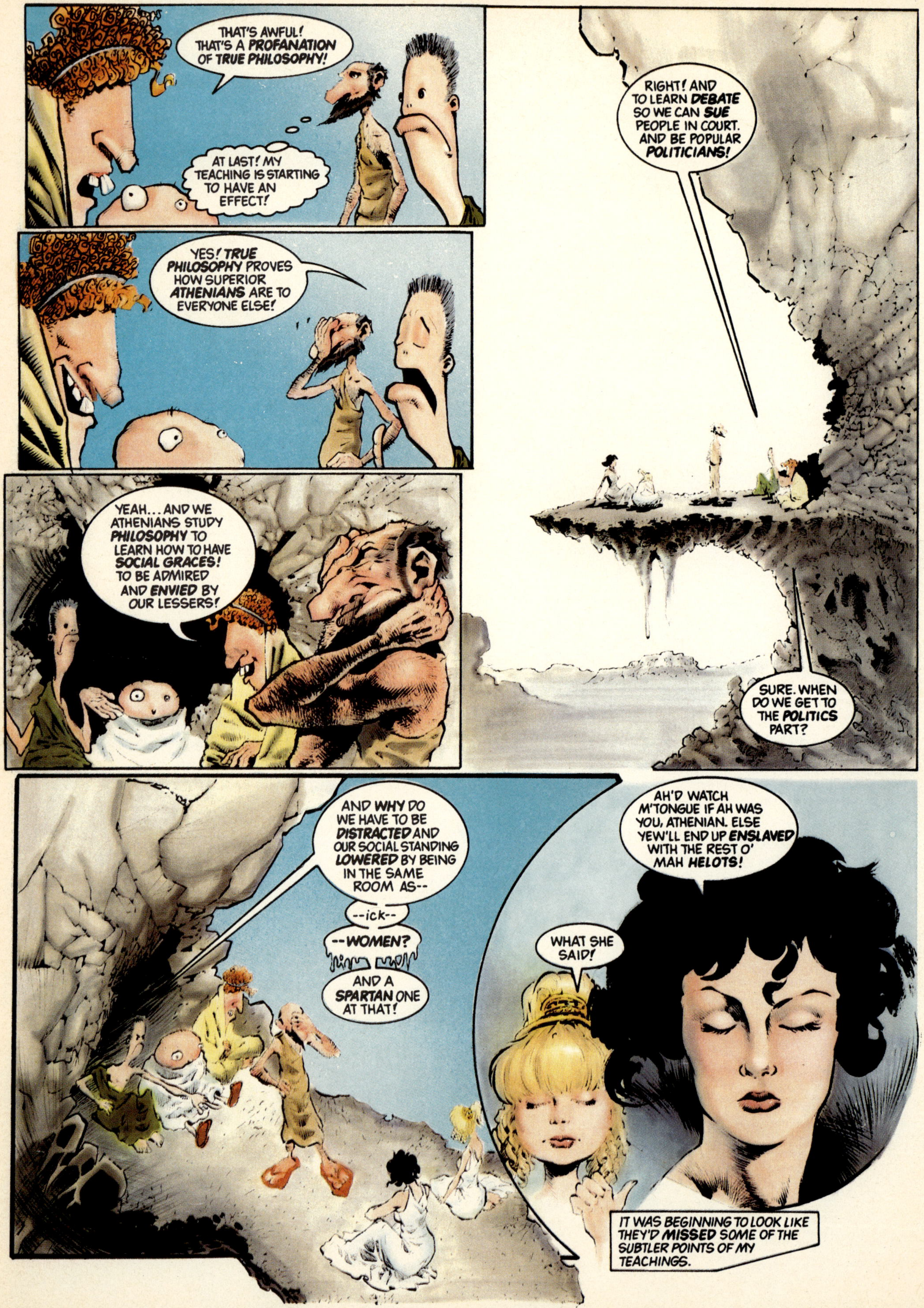
THAT'S AWFUL! THAT'S A PROFANATION OF TRUE PHILOSOPHY!
AT LAST! MY TEACHING IS STARTING TO HAVE AN EFFECT!
YES! TRUE PHILOSOPHY PROVES HOW SUPERIOR ATHENIANS ARE TO EVERYONE ELSE!
YEAH... AND WE ATHENIANS STUDY PHILOSOPHY TO LEARN HOW TO HAVE SOCIAL GRACES! TO BE ADMIRED AND ENVIED BY OUR LESSERS!
RIGHT! AND TO LEARN DEBATE SO WE CAN SUE PEOPLE IN COURT. AND BE POPULAR POLITICIANS!
SURE. WHEN DO WE GET TO THE POLITICS PART?
AND WHY DO WE HAVE TO BE DISTRACTED AND OUR SOCIAL STANDING LOWERED BY BEING IN THE SAME ROOM AS--
--ick--
--WOMEN?
AND A SPARTAN ONE AT THAT!
AH'D WATCH M'TONGUE IF AH WAS YOU, ATHENIAN. ELSE YEW'LL END UP ENSLAVED WITH THE REST O' MAH HELOTS!
WHAT SHE SAID!
IT WAS BEGINNING TO LOOK LIKE THEY'D MISSED SOME OF THE SUBTLER POINTS OF MY TEACHINGS.

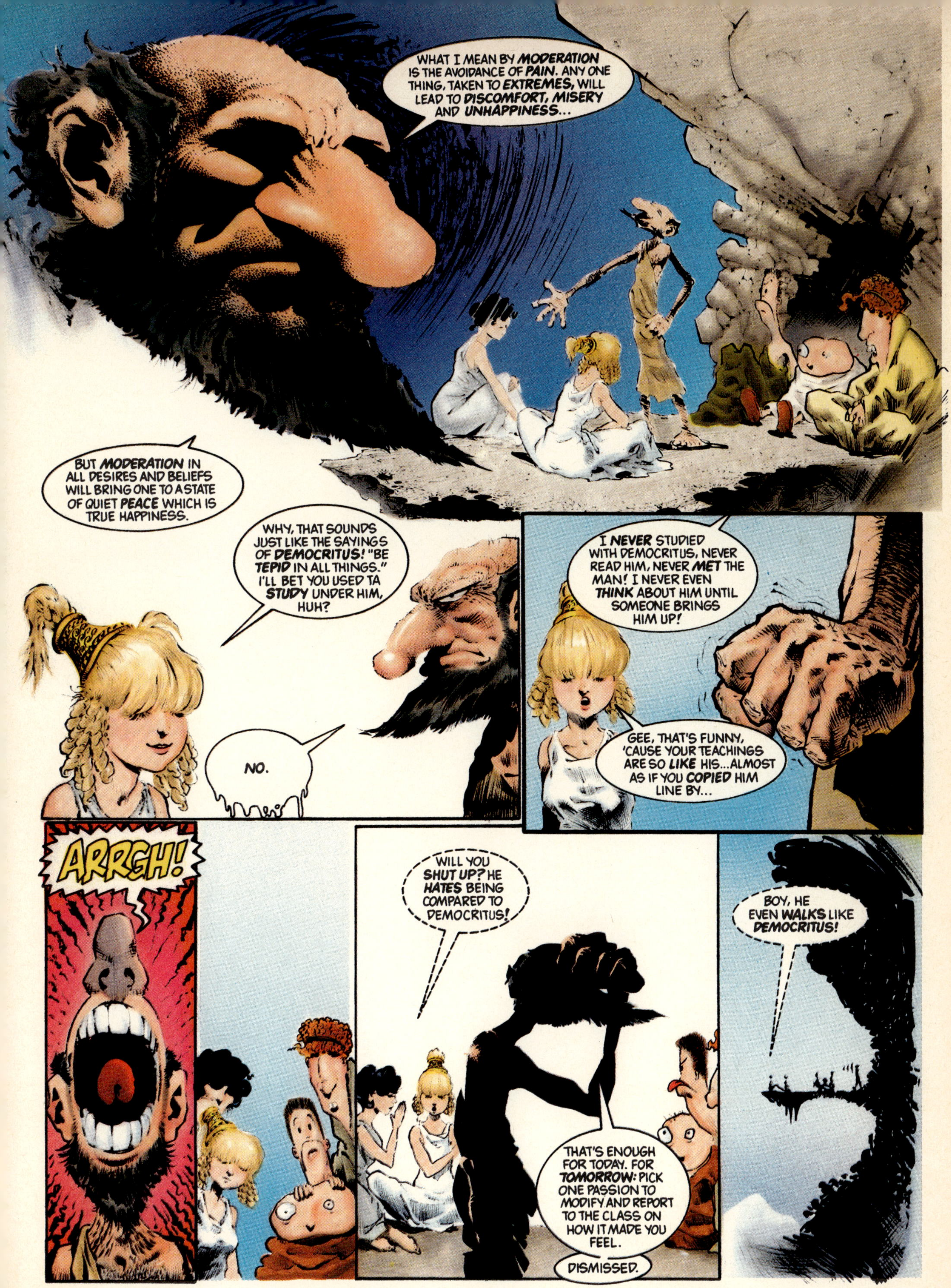
WHAT I MEAN BY MODERATION IS THE AVOIDANCE OF PAIN. ANY ONE THING, TAKEN TO EXTREMES, WILL LEAD TO DISCOMFORT, MISERY AND UNHAPPINESS...
BUT MODERATION IN ALL DESIRES AND BELIEFS WILL BRING ONE TO A STATE OF QUIET PEACE WHICH IS TRUE HAPPINESS.
WHY, THAT SOUNDS JUST LIKE THE SAYINGS OF DEMOCRITUS! "BE TEPID IN ALL THINGS." I'LL BET YOU USED TA STUDY UNDER HIM, HUH?
NO.
I NEVER STUDIED WITH DEMOCRITUS, NEVER READ HIM, NEVER MET THE MAN! I NEVER EVEN THINK ABOUT HIM UNTIL SOMEONE BRINGS HIM UP!
GEE, THAT'S FUNNY, 'CAUSE YOUR TEACHINGS ARE SO LIKE HIS...ALMOST AS IF YOU COPIED HIM LINE BY...
ARRGH!
WILL YOU SHUT UP? HE HATES BEING COMPARED TO DEMOCRITUS!
THAT'S ENOUGH FOR TODAY. FOR TOMORROW: PICK ONE PASSION TO MODIFY AND REPORT TO THE CLASS ON HOW IT MADE YOU FEEL.
DISMISSED.
BOY, HE EVEN WALKS LIKE DEMOCRITUS!

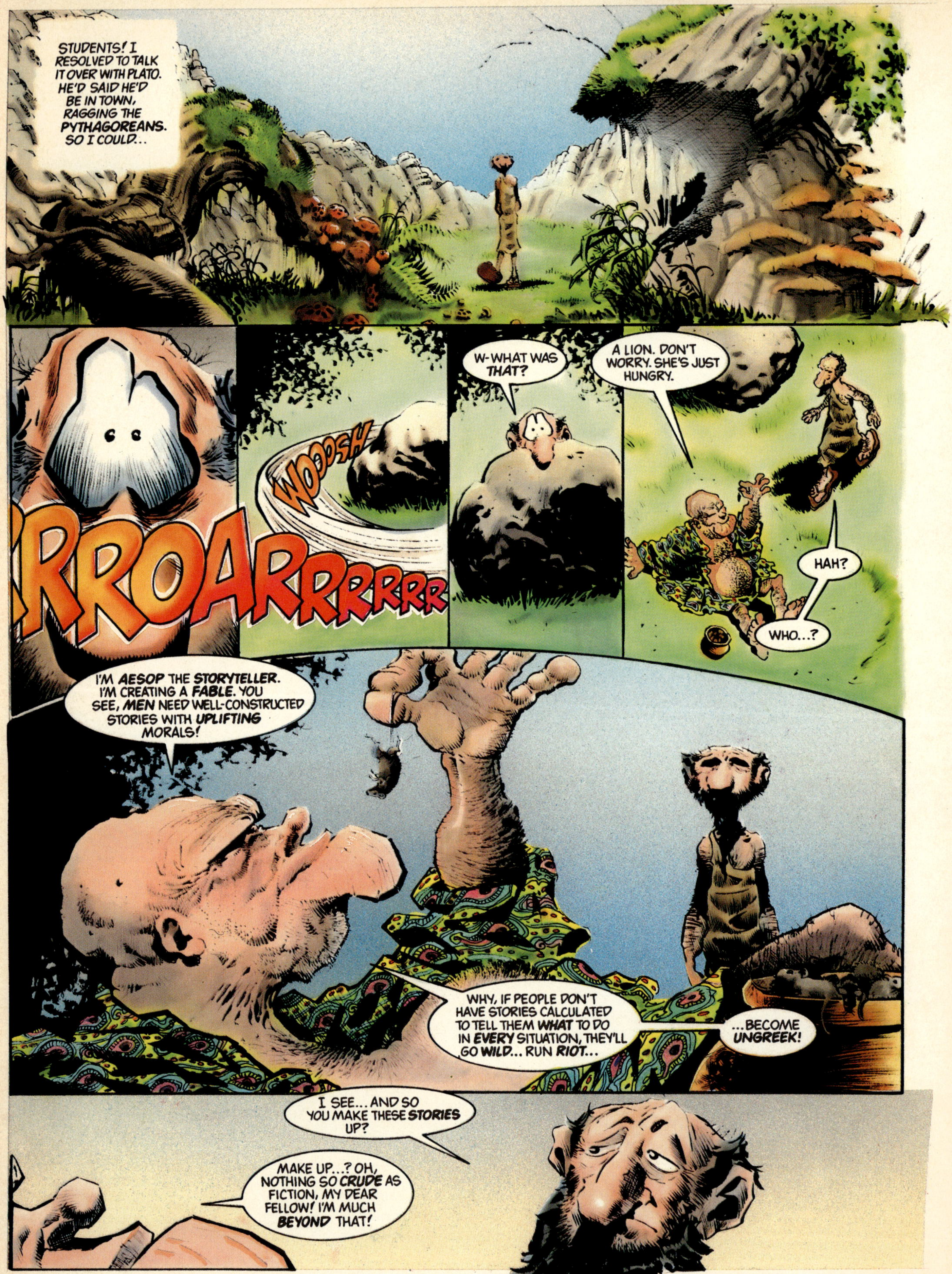
STUDENTS! I RESOLVED TO TALK IT OVER WITH PLATO. HE'D SAID HE'D BE IN TOWN, RAGGING THE PYTHAGOREANS. SO I COULD...
RROARRRRRR
WOOOSH
W-WHAT WAS THAT?
A LION. DON'T WORRY. SHE'S JUST HUNGRY.
HAH?
WHO...?
I'M AESOP THE STORYTELLER. I'M CREATING A FABLE. YOU SEE, MEN NEED WELL-CONSTRUCTED STORIES WITH UPLIFTING MORALS!
WHY, IF PEOPLE DON'T HAVE STORIES CALCULATED TO TELL THEM WHAT TO DO IN EVERY SITUATION, THEY'LL GO WILD... RUN RIOT...
...BECOME UNGREEK!
I SEE... AND SO YOU MAKE THESE STORIES UP?
MAKE UP...? OH, NOTHING SO CRUDE AS FICTION, MY DEAR FELLOW! I'M MUCH BEYOND THAT!

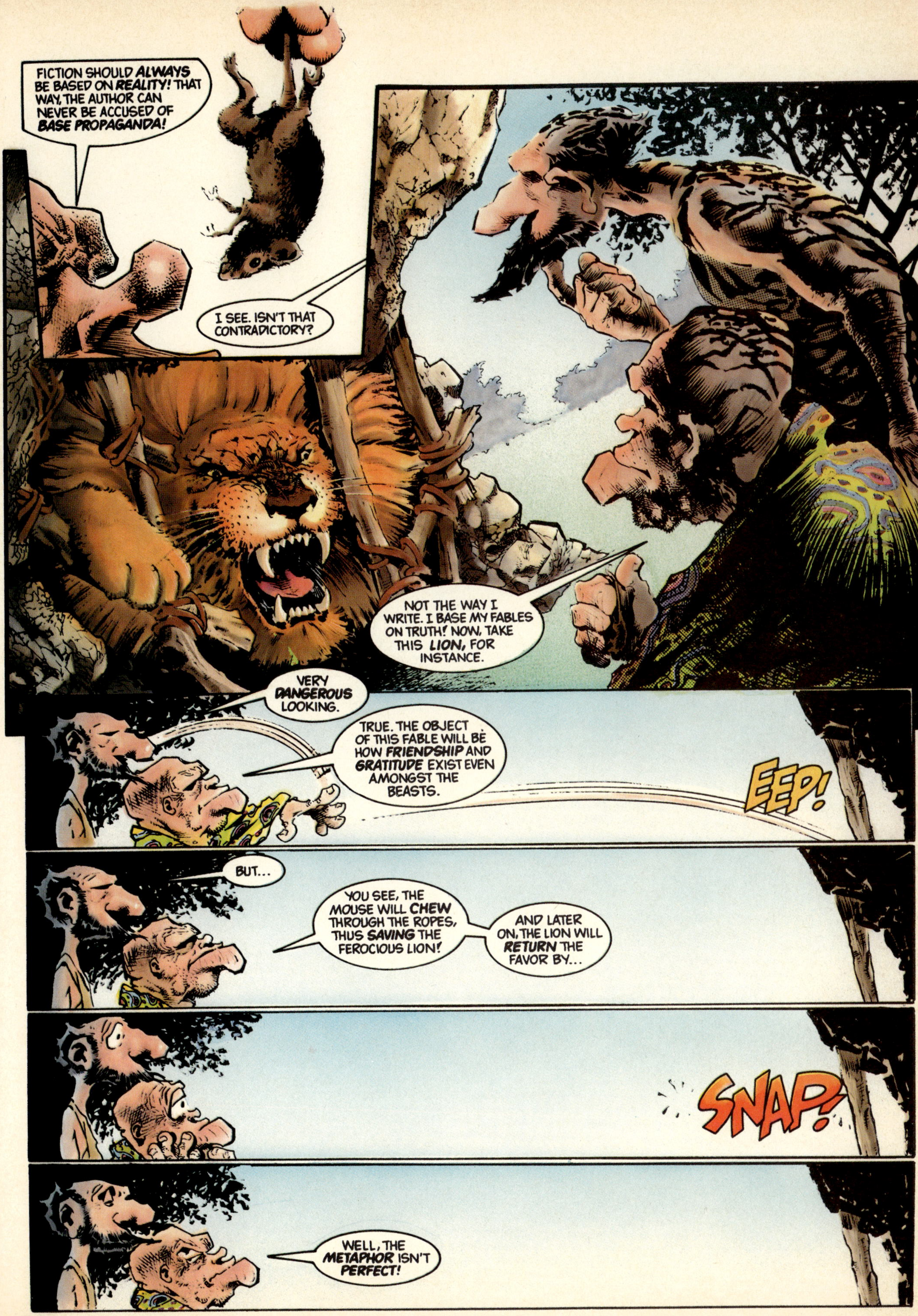

FICTION SHOULD **ALWAYS** BE BASED ON **REALITY!** THAT WAY, THE AUTHOR CAN NEVER BE ACCUSED OF ***BASE PROPAGANDA!***
I SEE. ISN'T THAT CONTRADICTORY?
NOT THE WAY I WRITE. I BASE MY FABLES ON TRUTH! NOW, TAKE THIS **LION,** FOR INSTANCE.
VERY **DANGEROUS** LOOKING.
TRUE. THE OBJECT OF THIS FABLE WILL BE HOW **FRIENDSHIP** AND **GRATITUDE** EXIST EVEN AMONGST THE BEASTS.
EEP!
BUT...
YOU SEE, THE MOUSE WILL **CHEW** THROUGH THE ROPES, THUS **SAVING** THE FEROCIOUS LION!
AND LATER ON, THE LION WILL **RETURN** THE FAVOR BY...
SNAP!
WELL, THE **METAPHOR** ISN'T **PERFECT!**

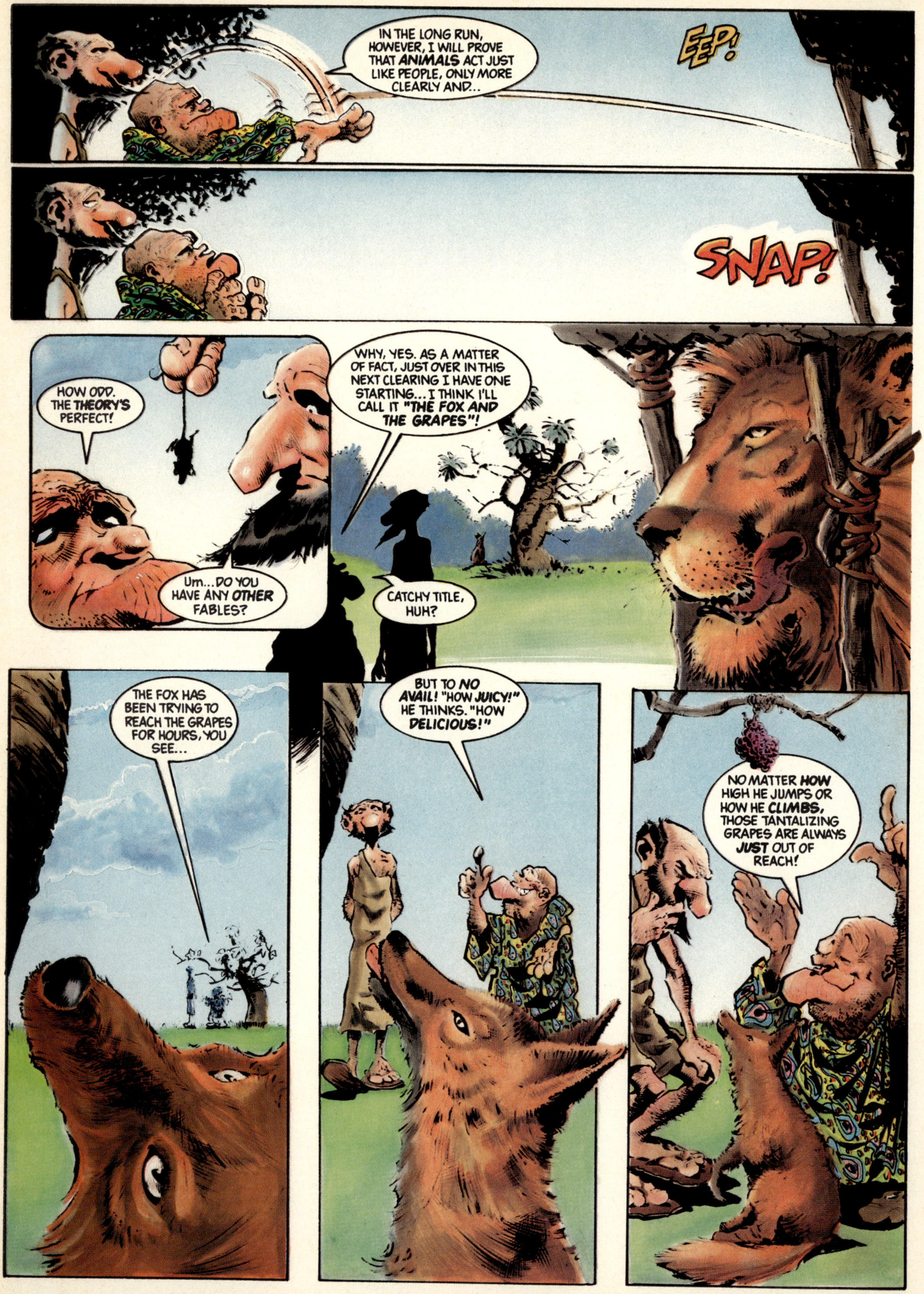
IN THE LONG RUN, HOWEVER, I WILL PROVE THAT ANIMALS ACT JUST LIKE PEOPLE, ONLY MORE CLEARLY AND...
EEP!
SNAP!
HOW ODD. THE THEORY'S PERFECT!
Um...DO YOU HAVE ANY OTHER FABLES?
WHY, YES. AS A MATTER OF FACT, JUST OVER IN THIS NEXT CLEARING I HAVE ONE STARTING... I THINK I'LL CALL IT "THE FOX AND THE GRAPES"!
CATCHY TITLE, HUH?
THE FOX HAS BEEN TRYING TO REACH THE GRAPES FOR HOURS, YOU SEE...
BUT TO NO AVAIL! "HOW JUICY!" HE THINKS. "HOW DELICIOUS!"
NO MATTER HOW HIGH HE JUMPS OR HOW HE CLIMBS, THOSE TANTALIZING GRAPES ARE ALWAYS JUST OUT OF REACH!

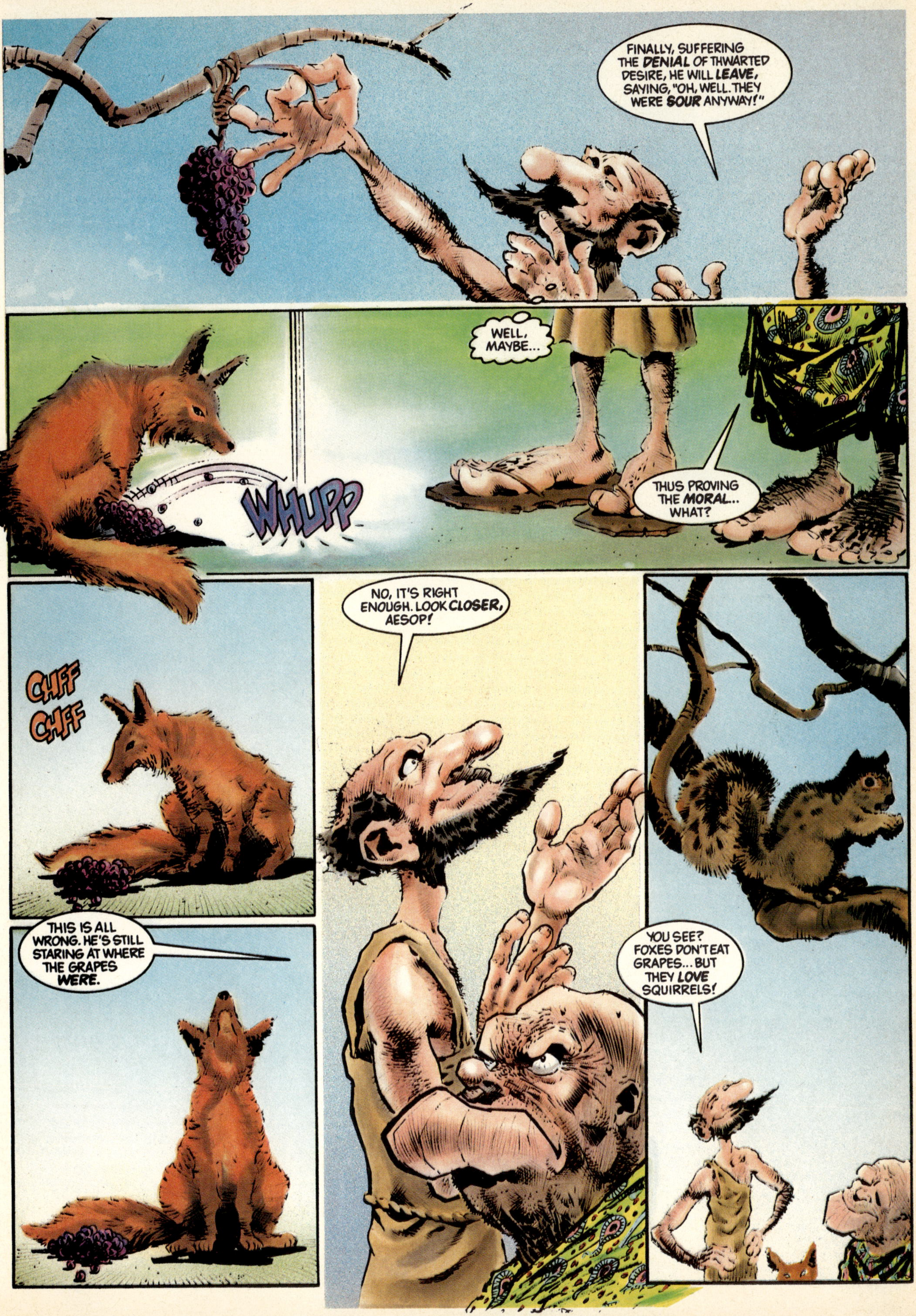
FINALLY, SUFFERING THE DENIAL OF THWARTED DESIRE, HE WILL LEAVE, SAYING, "OH, WELL. THEY WERE SOUR ANYWAY!"
WELL, MAYBE...
WHUPP
THUS PROVING THE MORAL... WHAT?
CHFF CHFF
THIS IS ALL WRONG. HE'S STILL STARING AT WHERE THE GRAPES WERE.
NO, IT'S RIGHT ENOUGH. LOOK CLOSER, AESOP!
YOU SEE? FOXES DON'T EAT GRAPES... BUT THEY LOVE SQUIRRELS!

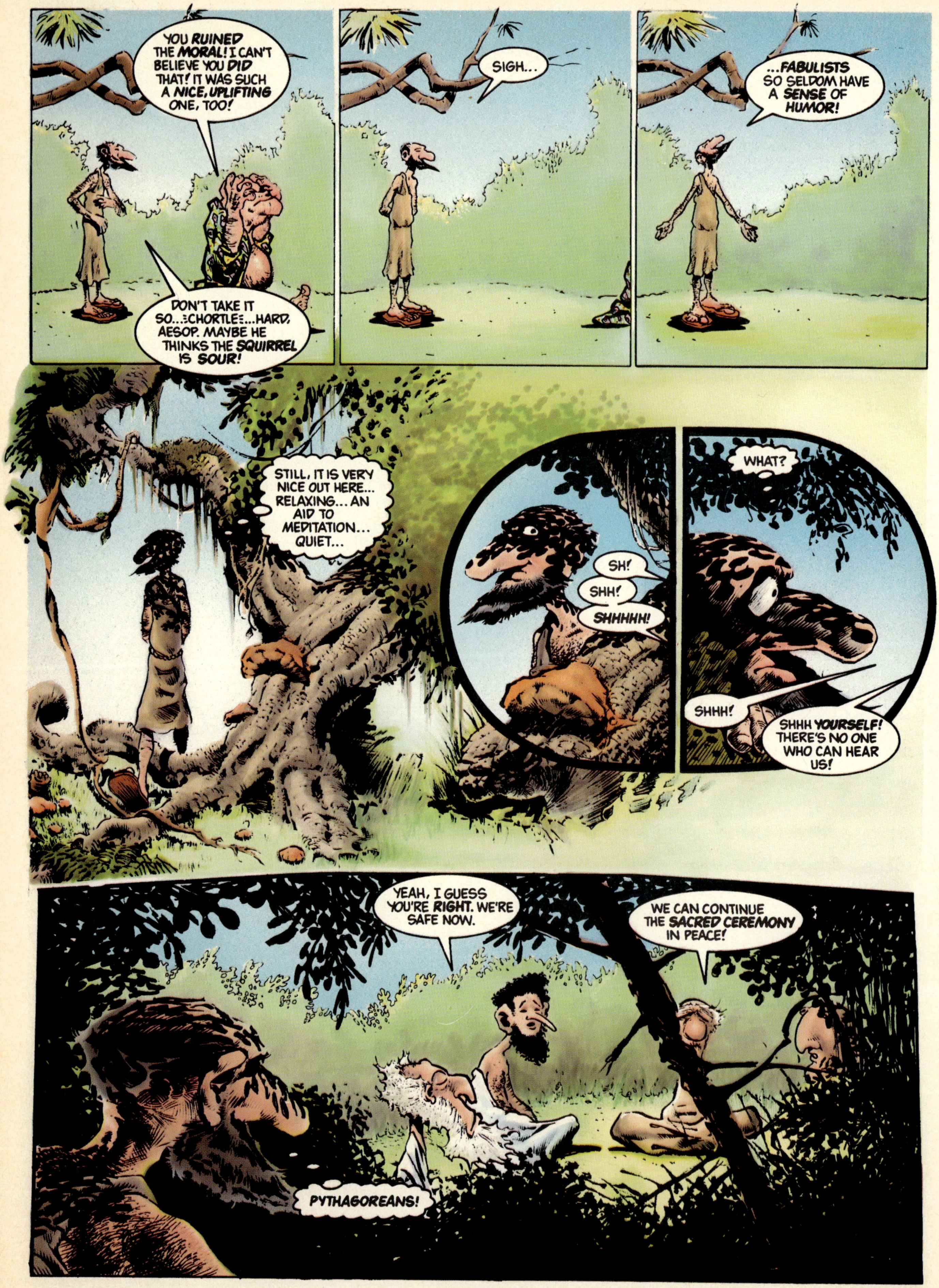
YOU RUINED THE MORAL! I CAN'T BELIEVE YOU DID THAT! IT WAS SUCH A NICE, UPLIFTING ONE, TOO!
DON'T TAKE IT SO...CHORTLE...HARD, AESOP. MAYBE HE THINKS THE SQUIRREL IS SOUR!
SIGH...
...FABULISTS SO SELDOM HAVE A SENSE OF HUMOR!
STILL, IT IS VERY NICE OUT HERE... RELAXING... AN AID TO MEDITATION... QUIET...
SH!
SHH!
SHHHHH!
WHAT?
SHHH!
SHHH YOURSELF! THERE'S NO ONE WHO CAN HEAR US!
YEAH, I GUESS YOU'RE RIGHT. WE'RE SAFE NOW.
WE CAN CONTINUE THE SACRED CEREMONY IN PEACE!
PYTHAGOREANS!

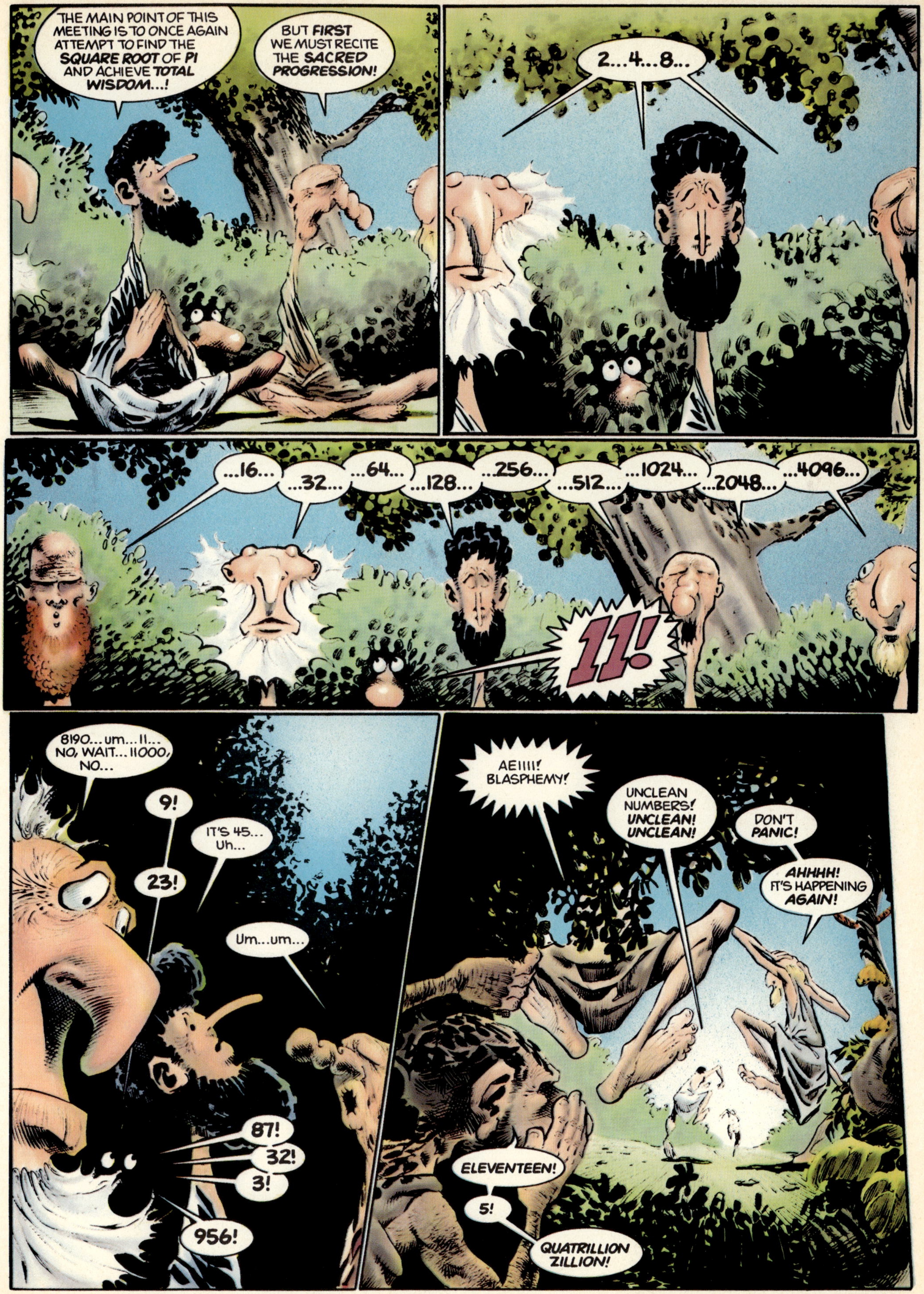
THE MAIN POINT OF THIS MEETING IS TO ONCE AGAIN ATTEMPT TO FIND THE SQUARE ROOT OF PI AND ACHIEVE TOTAL WISDOM...!
BUT FIRST WE MUST RECITE THE SACRED PROGRESSION!
2...4...8...
...16...
...32...
...64...
...128...
...256...
...512...
...1024...
...2048...
...4096...
11!
8190...um...11... NO, WAIT...11000, NO...
9!
IT'S 45... Uh...
23!
Um...um...
87!
32!
3!
956!
AEIIII! BLASPHEMY!
UNCLEAN NUMBERS! UNCLEAN! UNCLEAN!
DON'T PANIC!
AHHHH! IT'S HAPPENING AGAIN!
ELEVENTEEN!
5!
QUATRILLION ZILLION!

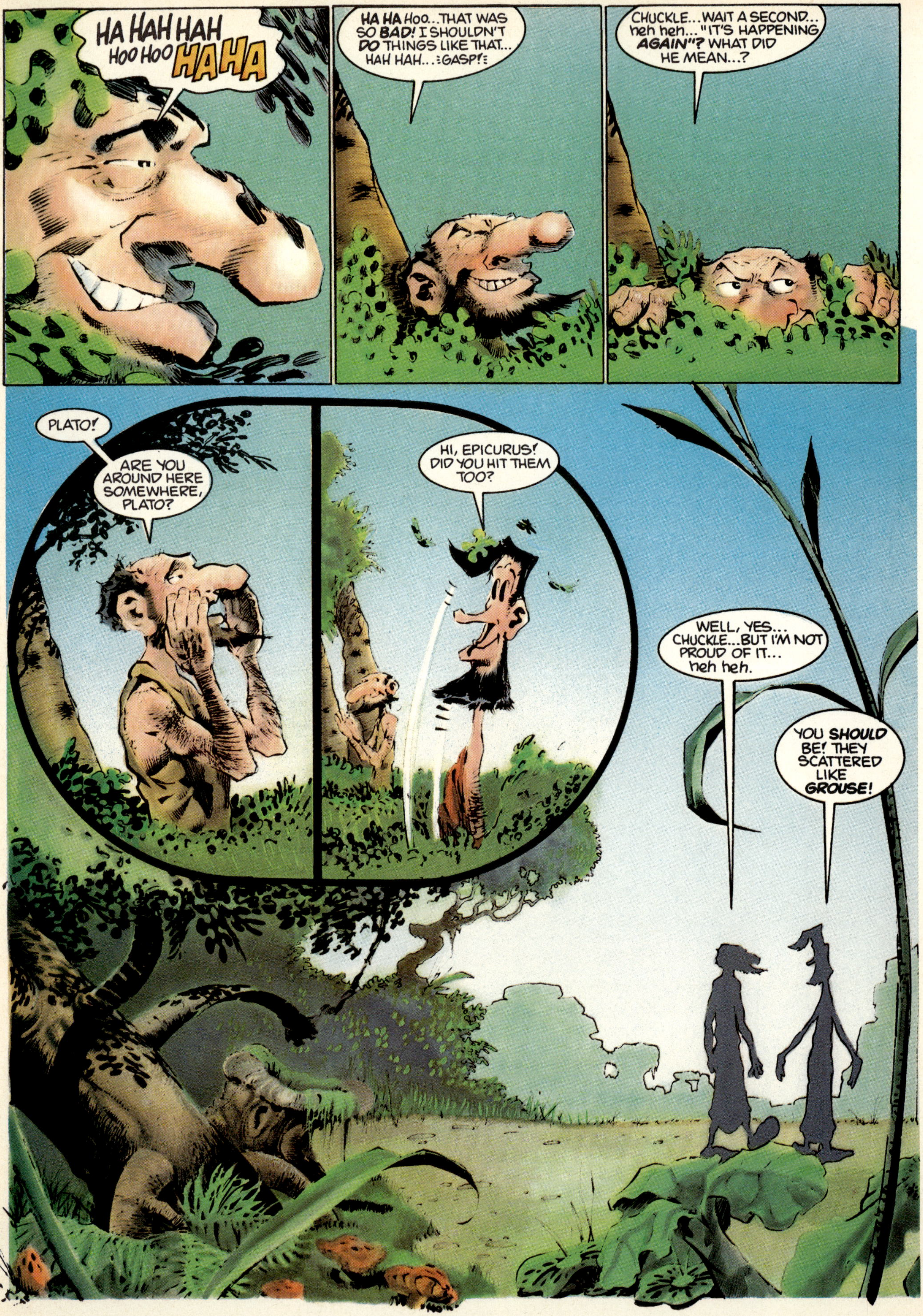
HA HAH HAH HOO HOO HAHA
HA HA HOO... THAT WAS SO BAD! I SHOULDN'T DO THINGS LIKE THAT... HAH HAH... GASP!
CHUCKLE... WAIT A SECOND... heh heh... "IT'S HAPPENING AGAIN"? WHAT DID HE MEAN...?
PLATO!
ARE YOU AROUND HERE SOMEWHERE, PLATO?
HI, EPICURUS! DID YOU HIT THEM TOO?
WELL, YES... CHUCKLE... BUT I'M NOT PROUD OF IT... heh heh.
YOU SHOULD BE! THEY SCATTERED LIKE GROUSE!

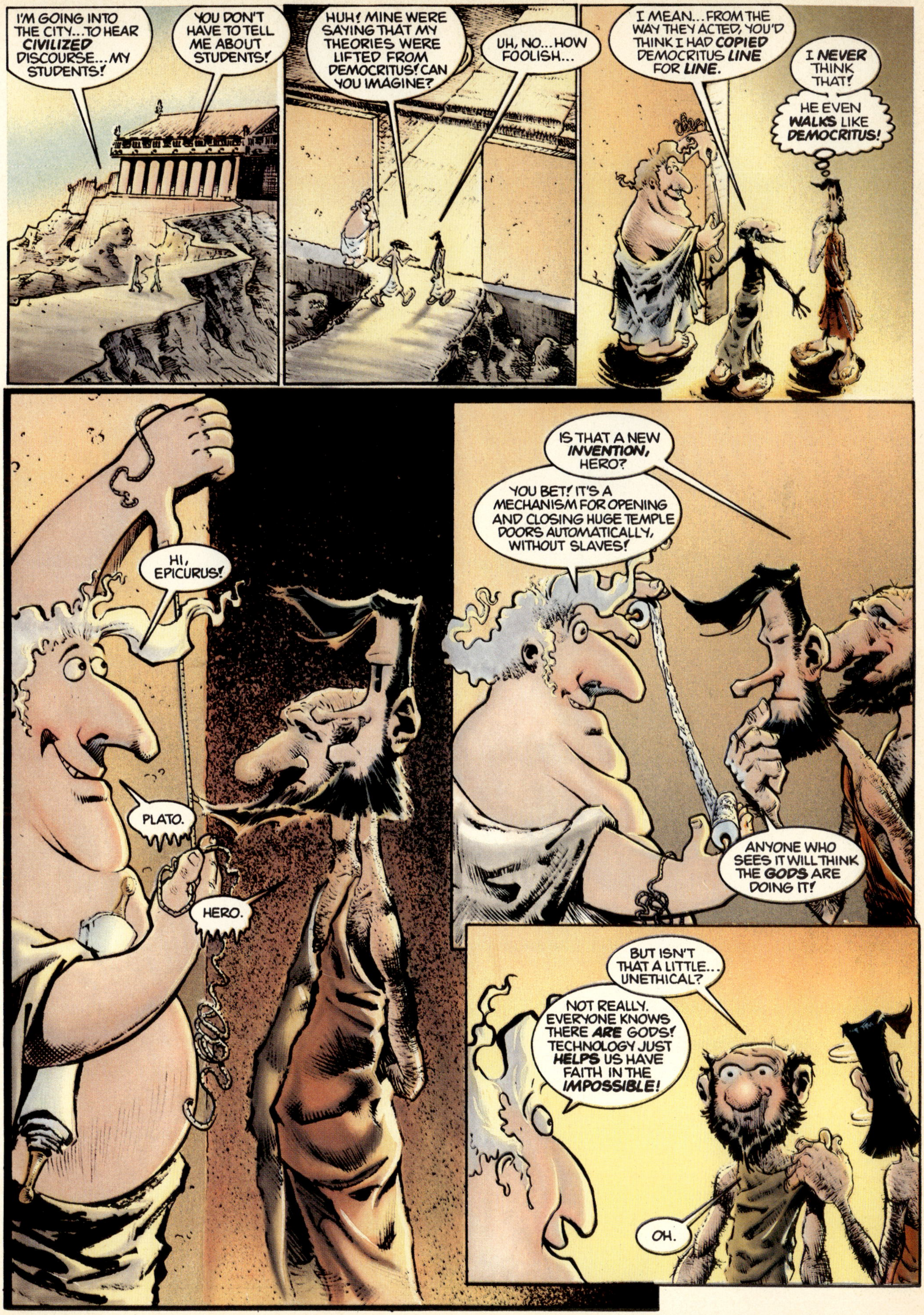
I'M GOING INTO THE CITY...TO HEAR CIVILIZED DISCOURSE...MY STUDENTS!
YOU DON'T HAVE TO TELL ME ABOUT STUDENTS!
HUH! MINE WERE SAYING THAT MY THEORIES WERE LIFTED FROM DEMOCRITUS! CAN YOU IMAGINE?
UH, NO...HOW FOOLISH...
I MEAN...FROM THE WAY THEY ACTED, YOU'D THINK I HAD COPIED DEMOCRITUS LINE FOR LINE.
I NEVER THINK THAT!
HE EVEN WALKS LIKE DEMOCRITUS!
HI, EPICURUS!
PLATO.
HERO.
IS THAT A NEW INVENTION, HERO?
YOU BET! IT'S A MECHANISM FOR OPENING AND CLOSING HUGE TEMPLE DOORS AUTOMATICALLY, WITHOUT SLAVES!
ANYONE WHO SEES IT WILL THINK THE GODS ARE DOING IT!
BUT ISN'T THAT A LITTLE... UNETHICAL?
NOT REALLY. EVERYONE KNOWS THERE ARE GODS! TECHNOLOGY JUST HELPS US HAVE FAITH IN THE IMPOSSIBLE!
OH.

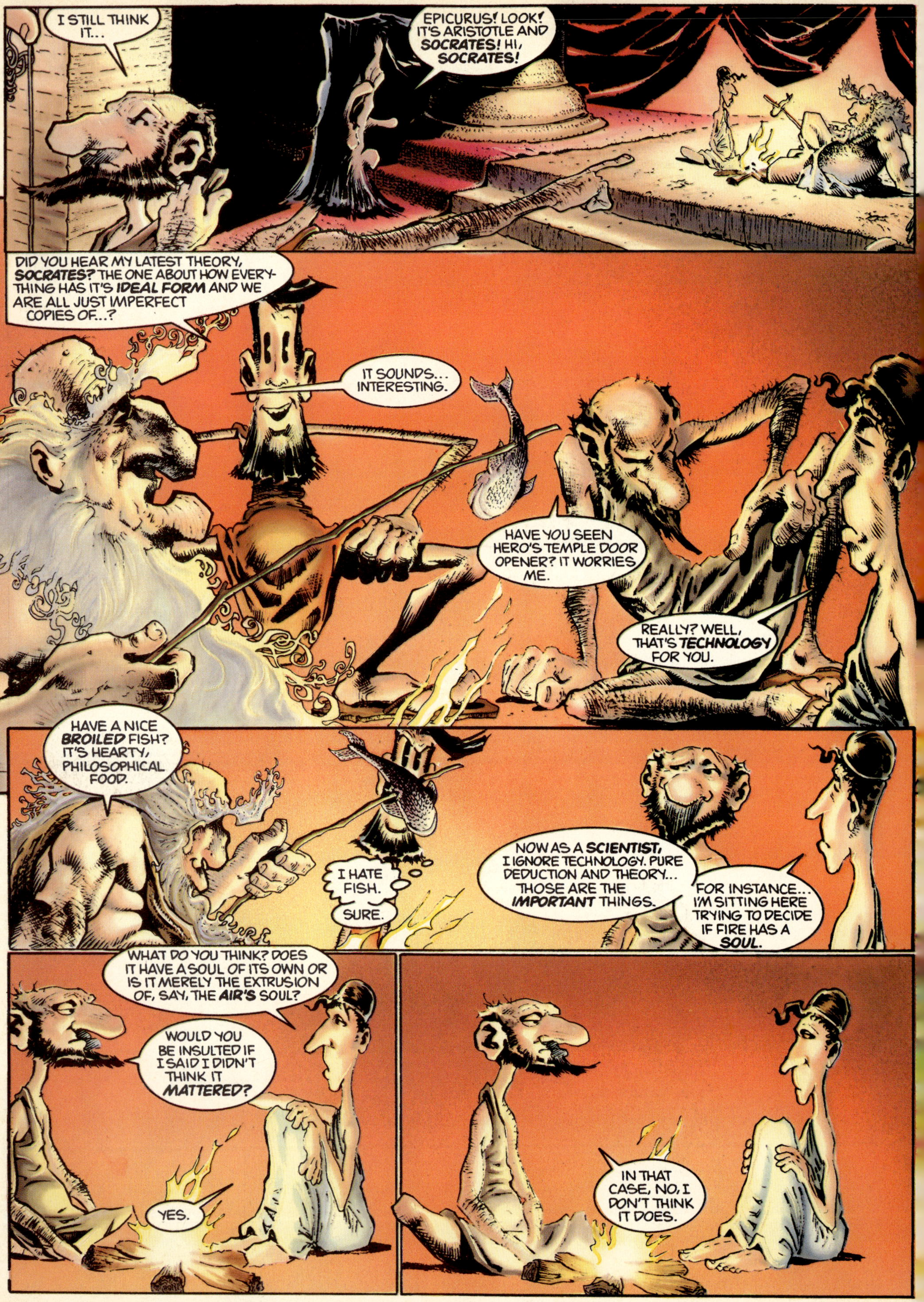
I STILL THINK IT...
EPICURUS! LOOK! IT'S ARISTOTLE AND SOCRATES! HI, SOCRATES!
DID YOU HEAR MY LATEST THEORY, SOCRATES? THE ONE ABOUT HOW EVERY-THING HAS IT'S IDEAL FORM AND WE ARE ALL JUST IMPERFECT COPIES OF...?
IT SOUNDS... INTERESTING.
HAVE YOU SEEN HERO'S TEMPLE DOOR OPENER? IT WORRIES ME.
REALLY? WELL, THAT'S TECHNOLOGY FOR YOU.
HAVE A NICE BROILED FISH? IT'S HEARTY, PHILOSOPHICAL FOOD.
I HATE FISH.
SURE.
NOW AS A SCIENTIST, I IGNORE TECHNOLOGY. PURE DEDUCTION AND THEORY... THOSE ARE THE IMPORTANT THINGS.
FOR INSTANCE... I'M SITTING HERE TRYING TO DECIDE IF FIRE HAS A SOUL.
WHAT DO YOU THINK? DOES IT HAVE A SOUL OF ITS OWN OR IS IT MERELY THE EXTRUSION OF, SAY, THE AIR'S SOUL?
WOULD YOU BE INSULTED IF I SAID I DIDN'T THINK IT MATTERED?
YES.
IN THAT CASE, NO, I DON'T THINK IT DOES.

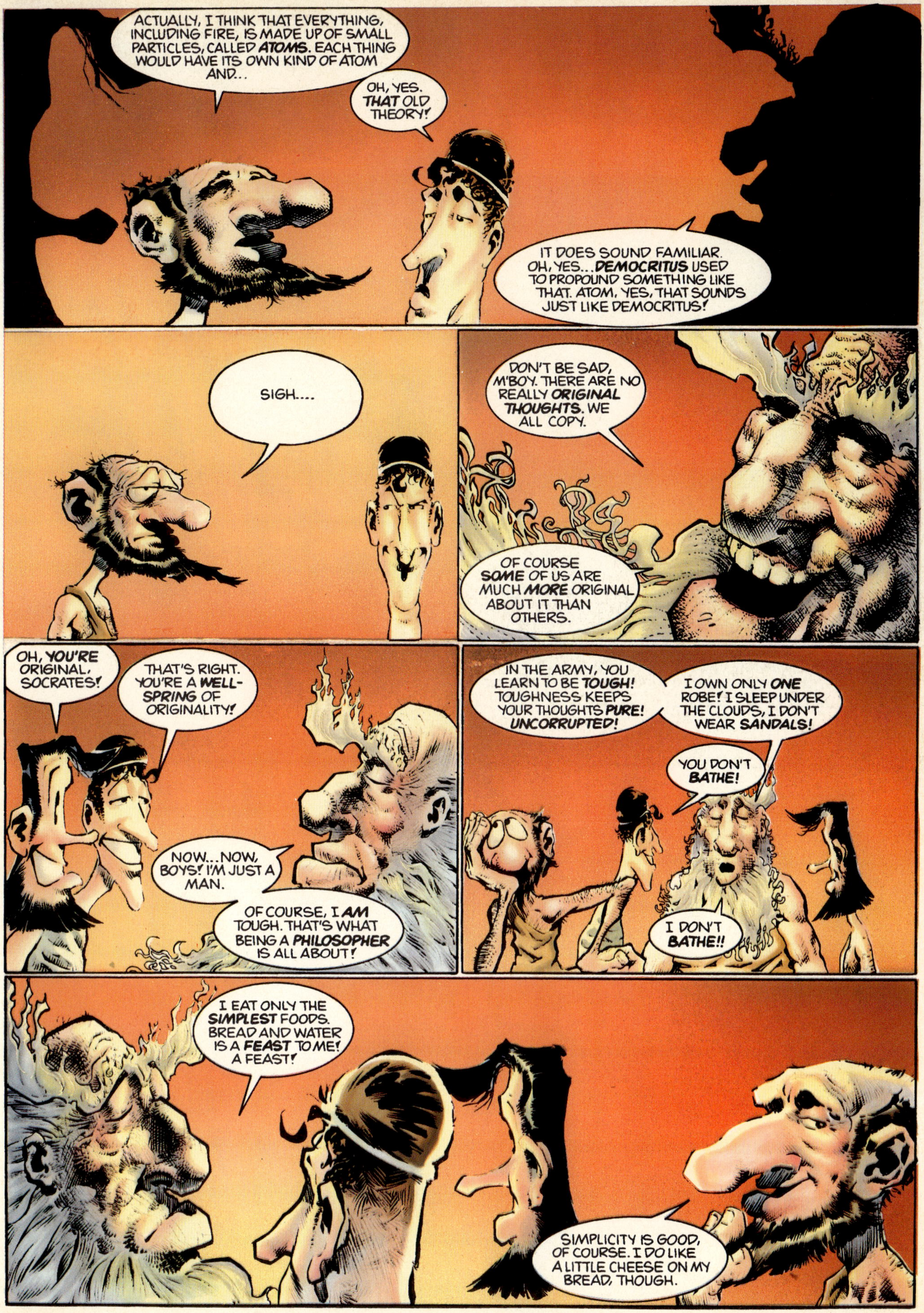
ACTUALLY, I THINK THAT EVERYTHING, INCLUDING FIRE, IS MADE UP OF SMALL PARTICLES, CALLED **ATOMS**. EACH THING WOULD HAVE ITS OWN KIND OF ATOM AND...
OH, YES. **THAT** OLD THEORY!
IT DOES SOUND FAMILIAR. OH, YES... **DEMOCRITUS** USED TO PROPOUND SOMETHING LIKE THAT. ATOM, YES, THAT SOUNDS JUST LIKE DEMOCRITUS!
SIGH....
DON'T BE SAD, M'BOY. THERE ARE NO REALLY **ORIGINAL THOUGHTS**. WE ALL COPY.
OF COURSE **SOME** OF US ARE MUCH **MORE** ORIGINAL ABOUT IT THAN OTHERS.
OH, **YOU'RE** ORIGINAL, SOCRATES!
THAT'S RIGHT. YOU'RE A **WELL-SPRING** OF ORIGINALITY!
NOW...NOW, BOYS! I'M JUST A MAN.
OF COURSE, I **AM** TOUGH. THAT'S WHAT BEING A **PHILOSOPHER** IS ALL ABOUT!
IN THE ARMY, YOU LEARN TO BE **TOUGH**! TOUGHNESS KEEPS YOUR THOUGHTS **PURE**! **UNCORRUPTED!**
I OWN ONLY **ONE** ROBE! I SLEEP UNDER THE CLOUDS, I DON'T WEAR **SANDALS**!
YOU DON'T **BATHE**!
I DON'T **BATHE!!**
I EAT ONLY THE **SIMPLEST** FOODS. BREAD AND WATER IS A **FEAST** TO ME! A FEAST!
SIMPLICITY IS GOOD, OF COURSE. I DO LIKE A LITTLE CHEESE ON MY BREAD, THOUGH.

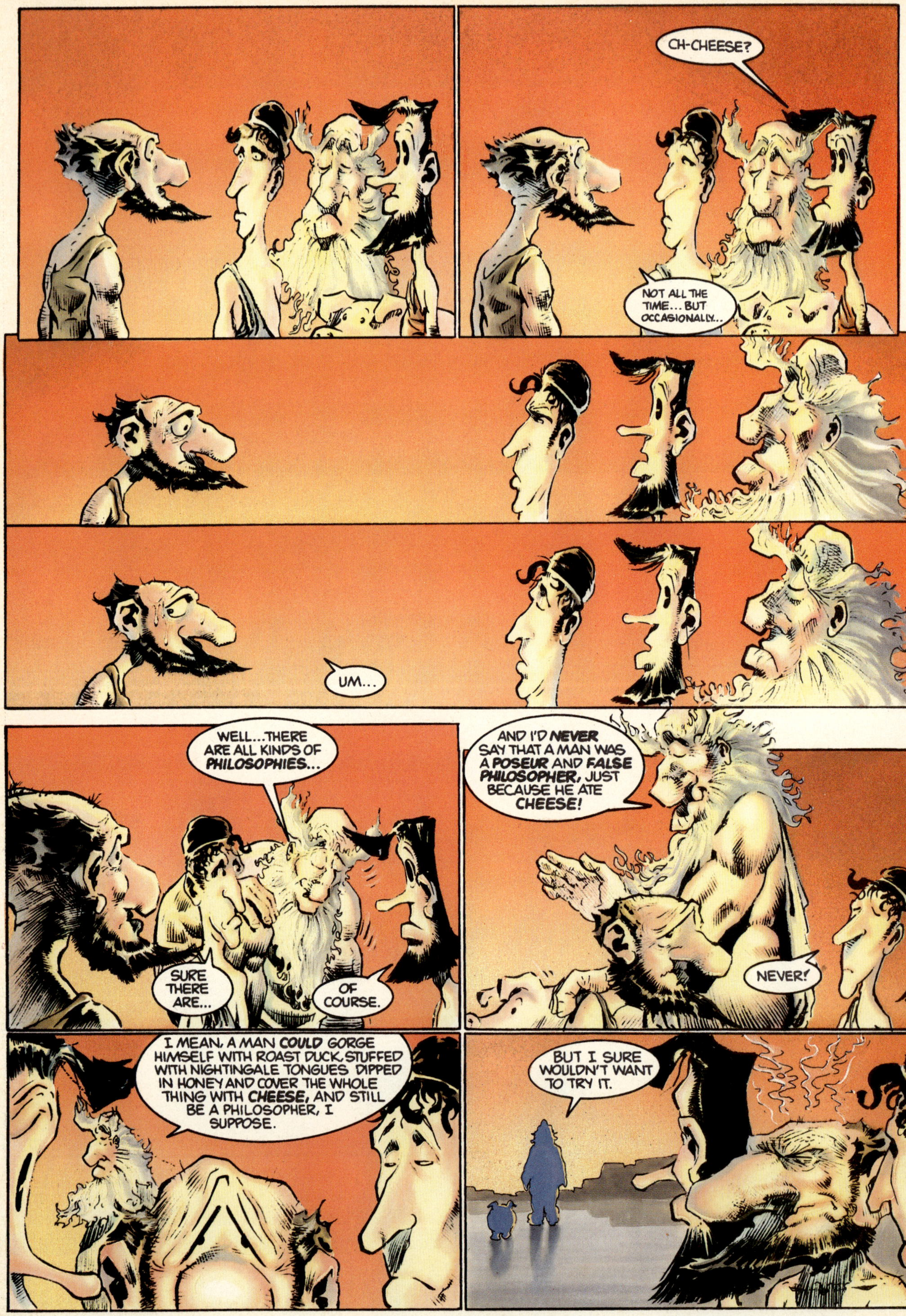
CH-CHEESE?
NOT ALL THE TIME... BUT OCCASIONALLY...
UM...
WELL...THERE ARE ALL KINDS OF **PHILOSOPHIES...**
SURE THERE ARE...
OF COURSE.
AND I'D **NEVER** SAY THAT A MAN WAS A **POSEUR** AND **FALSE PHILOSOPHER,** JUST BECAUSE HE ATE **CHEESE!**
NEVER!
I MEAN, A MAN **COULD** GORGE HIMSELF WITH ROAST DUCK, STUFFED WITH NIGHTINGALE TONGUES DIPPED IN HONEY AND COVER THE WHOLE THING WITH **CHEESE,** AND STILL BE A PHILOSOPHER, I SUPPOSE.
BUT I SURE WOULDN'T WANT TO TRY IT.

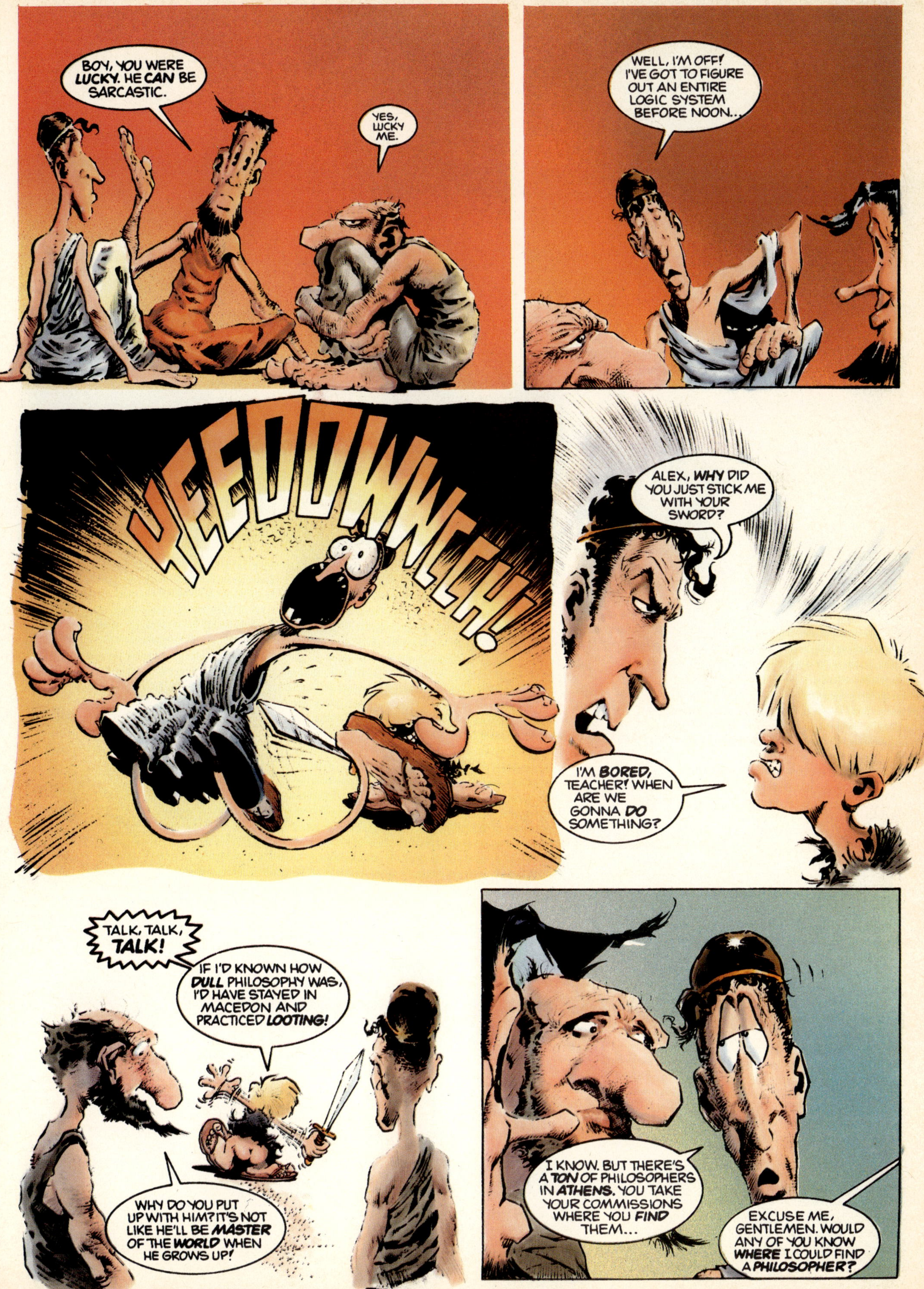
BOY, YOU WERE LUCKY. HE CAN BE SARCASTIC.
YES, LUCKY ME.
WELL, I'M OFF! I'VE GOT TO FIGURE OUT AN ENTIRE LOGIC SYSTEM BEFORE NOON...
YEEOOWNCH!
ALEX, WHY DID YOU JUST STICK ME WITH YOUR SWORD?
I'M BORED, TEACHER! WHEN ARE WE GONNA DO SOMETHING?
TALK, TALK, TALK!
IF I'D KNOWN HOW DULL PHILOSOPHY WAS, I'D HAVE STAYED IN MACEDON AND PRACTICED LOOTING!
WHY DO YOU PUT UP WITH HIM? IT'S NOT LIKE HE'LL BE MASTER OF THE WORLD WHEN HE GROWS UP!
I KNOW. BUT THERE'S A TON OF PHILOSOPHERS IN ATHENS. YOU TAKE YOUR COMMISSIONS WHERE YOU FIND THEM...
EXCUSE ME, GENTLEMEN. WOULD ANY OF YOU KNOW WHERE I COULD FIND A PHILOSOPHER?

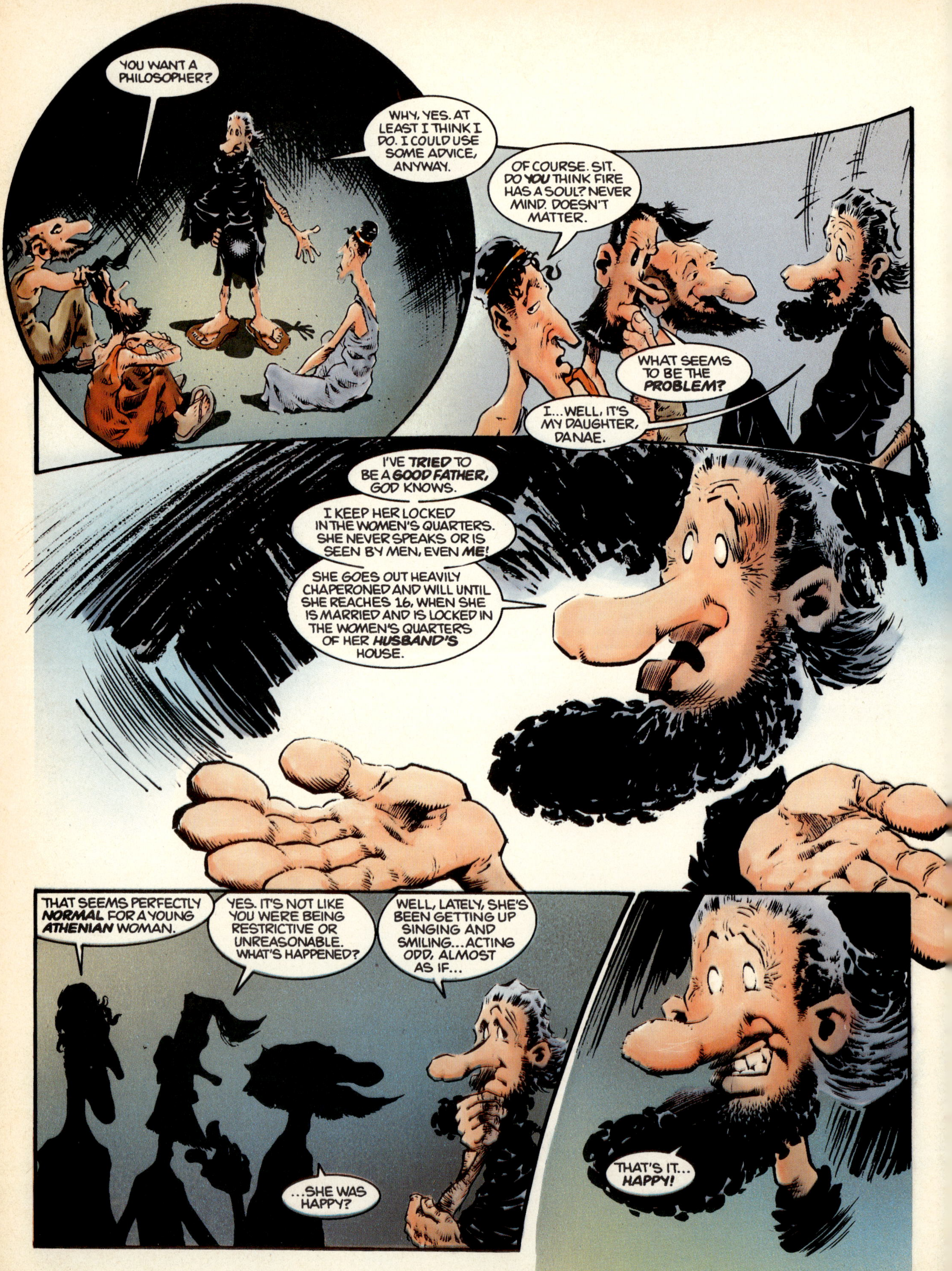
YOU WANT A PHILOSOPHER?
WHY, YES. AT LEAST I THINK I DO. I COULD USE SOME ADVICE, ANYWAY.
OF COURSE. SIT. DO YOU THINK FIRE HAS A SOUL? NEVER MIND. DOESN'T MATTER.
WHAT SEEMS TO BE THE PROBLEM?
I...WELL, IT'S MY DAUGHTER, DANAE.
I'VE TRIED TO BE A GOOD FATHER, GOD KNOWS.
I KEEP HER LOCKED IN THE WOMEN'S QUARTERS. SHE NEVER SPEAKS OR IS SEEN BY MEN, EVEN ME!
SHE GOES OUT HEAVILY CHAPERONED AND WILL UNTIL SHE REACHES 16, WHEN SHE IS MARRIED AND IS LOCKED IN THE WOMEN'S QUARTERS OF HER HUSBAND'S HOUSE.
THAT SEEMS PERFECTLY NORMAL FOR A YOUNG ATHENIAN WOMAN.
YES. IT'S NOT LIKE YOU WERE BEING RESTRICTIVE OR UNREASONABLE. WHAT'S HAPPENED?
WELL, LATELY, SHE'S BEEN GETTING UP SINGING AND SMILING... ACTING ODD, ALMOST AS IF...
...SHE WAS HAPPY?
THAT'S IT... HAPPY!

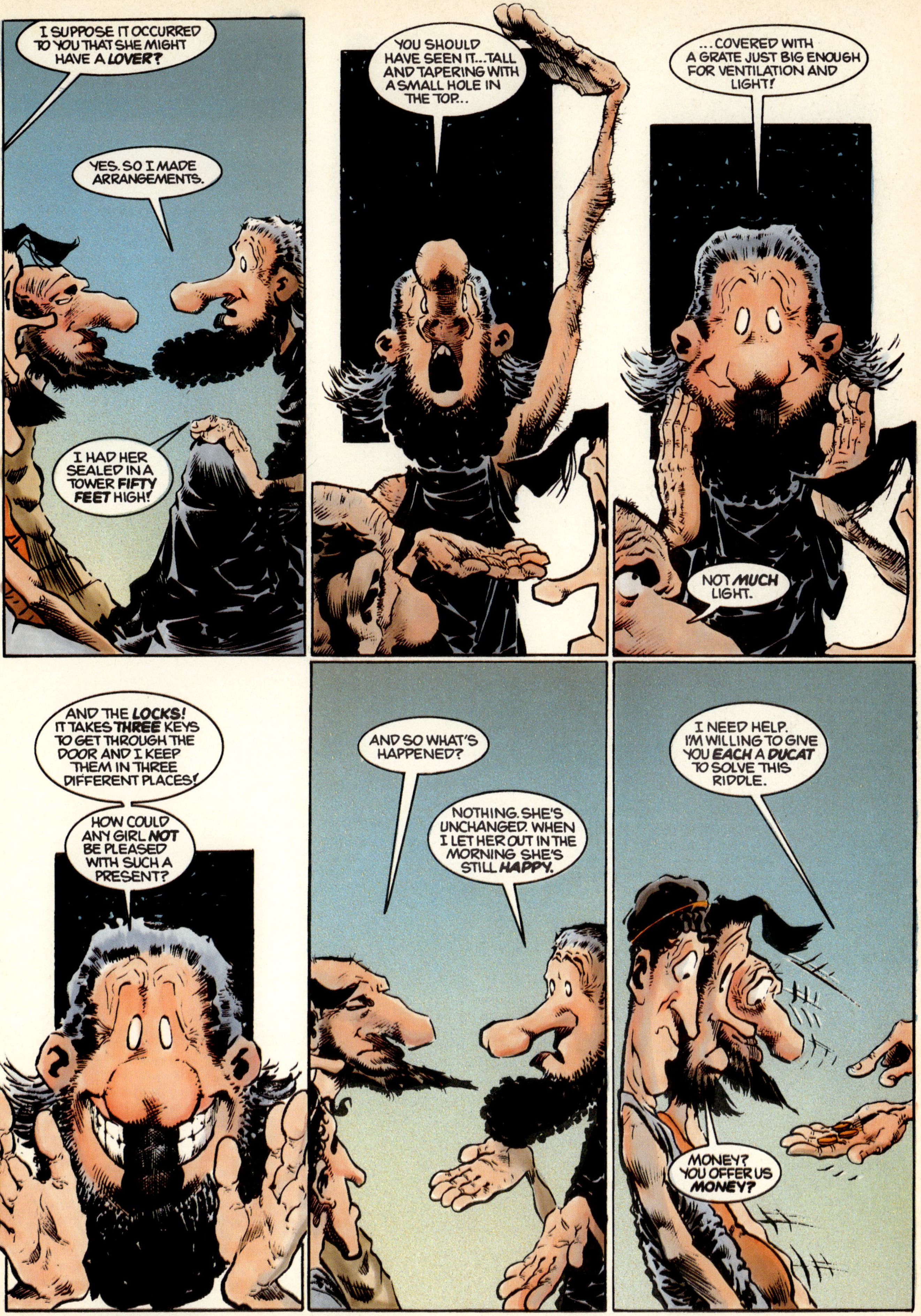
I SUPPOSE IT OCCURRED TO YOU THAT SHE MIGHT HAVE A LOVER?
YES. SO I MADE ARRANGEMENTS.
I HAD HER SEALED IN A TOWER FIFTY FEET HIGH!
YOU SHOULD HAVE SEEN IT...TALL AND TAPERING WITH A SMALL HOLE IN THE TOP...
...COVERED WITH A GRATE JUST BIG ENOUGH FOR VENTILATION AND LIGHT!
NOT MUCH LIGHT.
AND THE LOCKS! IT TAKES THREE KEYS TO GET THROUGH THE DOOR AND I KEEP THEM IN THREE DIFFERENT PLACES!
HOW COULD ANY GIRL NOT BE PLEASED WITH SUCH A PRESENT?
AND SO WHAT'S HAPPENED?
NOTHING. SHE'S UNCHANGED. WHEN I LET HER OUT IN THE MORNING SHE'S STILL HAPPY.
I NEED HELP. I'M WILLING TO GIVE YOU EACH A DUCAT TO SOLVE THIS RIDDLE.
MONEY? YOU OFFER US MONEY?

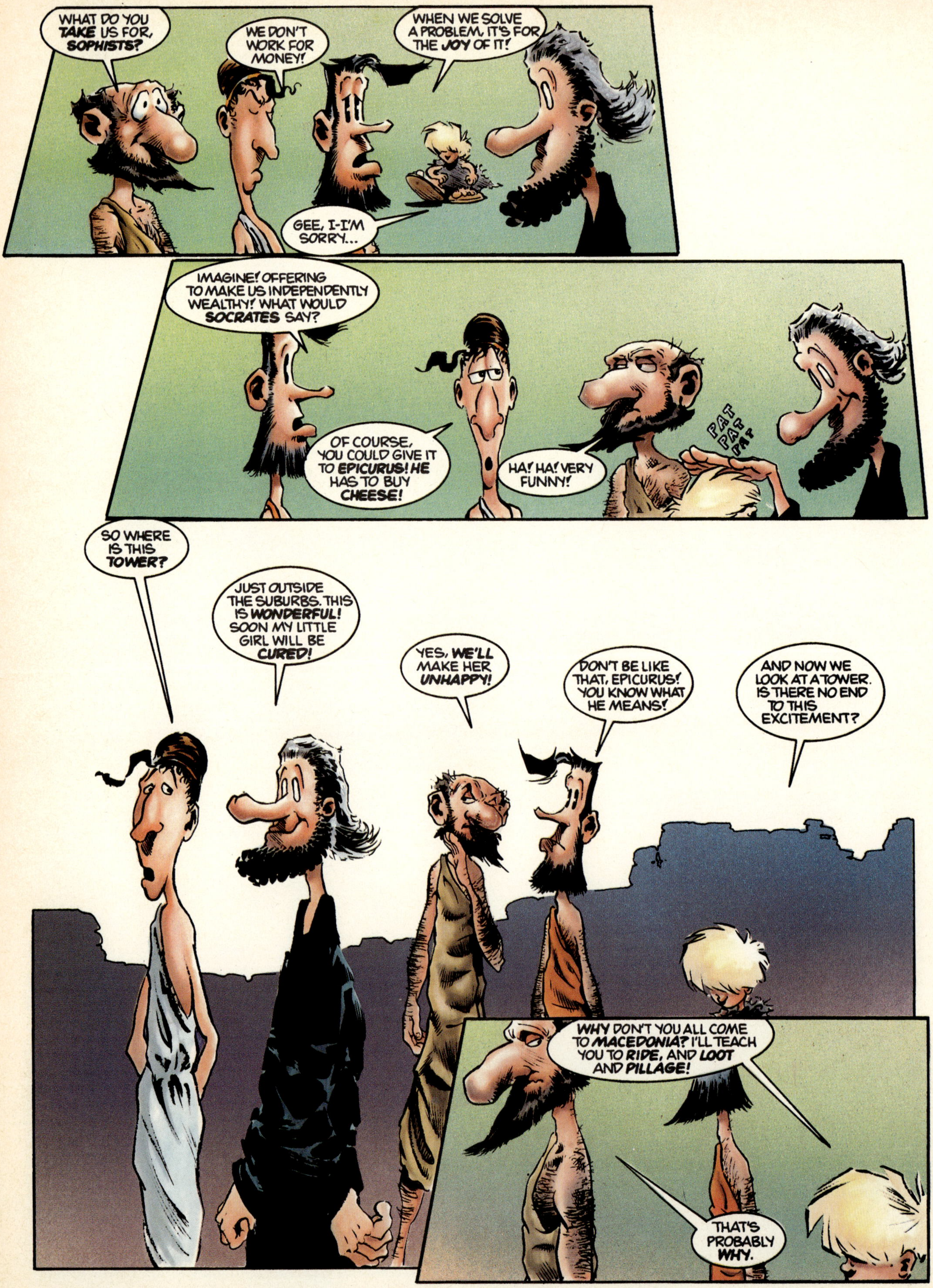
WHAT DO YOU TAKE US FOR, SOPHISTS?
WE DON'T WORK FOR MONEY!
WHEN WE SOLVE A PROBLEM, IT'S FOR THE JOY OF IT!
GEE, I-I'M SORRY...
IMAGINE! OFFERING TO MAKE US INDEPENDENTLY WEALTHY! WHAT WOULD SOCRATES SAY?
OF COURSE, YOU COULD GIVE IT TO EPICURUS! HE HAS TO BUY CHEESE!
HA! HA! VERY FUNNY!
PAT PAT PAT
SO WHERE IS THIS TOWER?
JUST OUTSIDE THE SUBURBS. THIS IS WONDERFUL! SOON MY LITTLE GIRL WILL BE CURED!
YES, WE'LL MAKE HER UNHAPPY!
DON'T BE LIKE THAT, EPICURUS! YOU KNOW WHAT HE MEANS!
AND NOW WE LOOK AT A TOWER. IS THERE NO END TO THIS EXCITEMENT?
WHY DON'T YOU ALL COME TO MACEDONIA? I'LL TEACH YOU TO RIDE, AND LOOT AND PILLAGE!
THAT'S PROBABLY WHY.

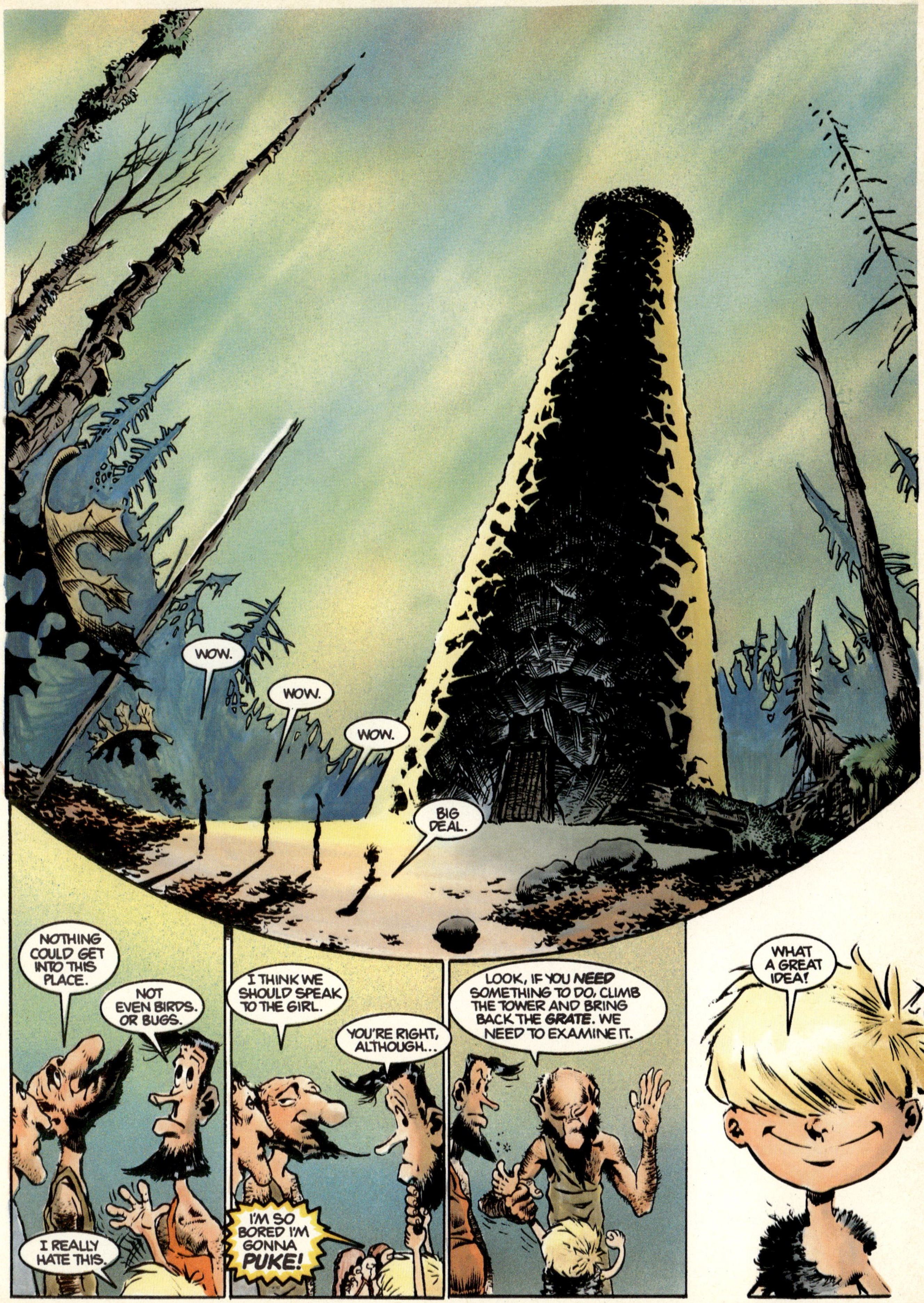
WOW.
WOW.
WOW.
BIG DEAL.
NOTHING COULD GET INTO THIS PLACE.
NOT EVEN BIRDS. OR BUGS.
I REALLY HATE THIS.
I THINK WE SHOULD SPEAK TO THE GIRL.
YOU'RE RIGHT, ALTHOUGH...
I'M SO BORED I'M GONNA **PUKE!**
LOOK, IF YOU **NEED** SOMETHING TO DO, CLIMB THE TOWER AND BRING BACK THE **GRATE**. WE NEED TO EXAMINE IT.
WHAT A GREAT IDEA!

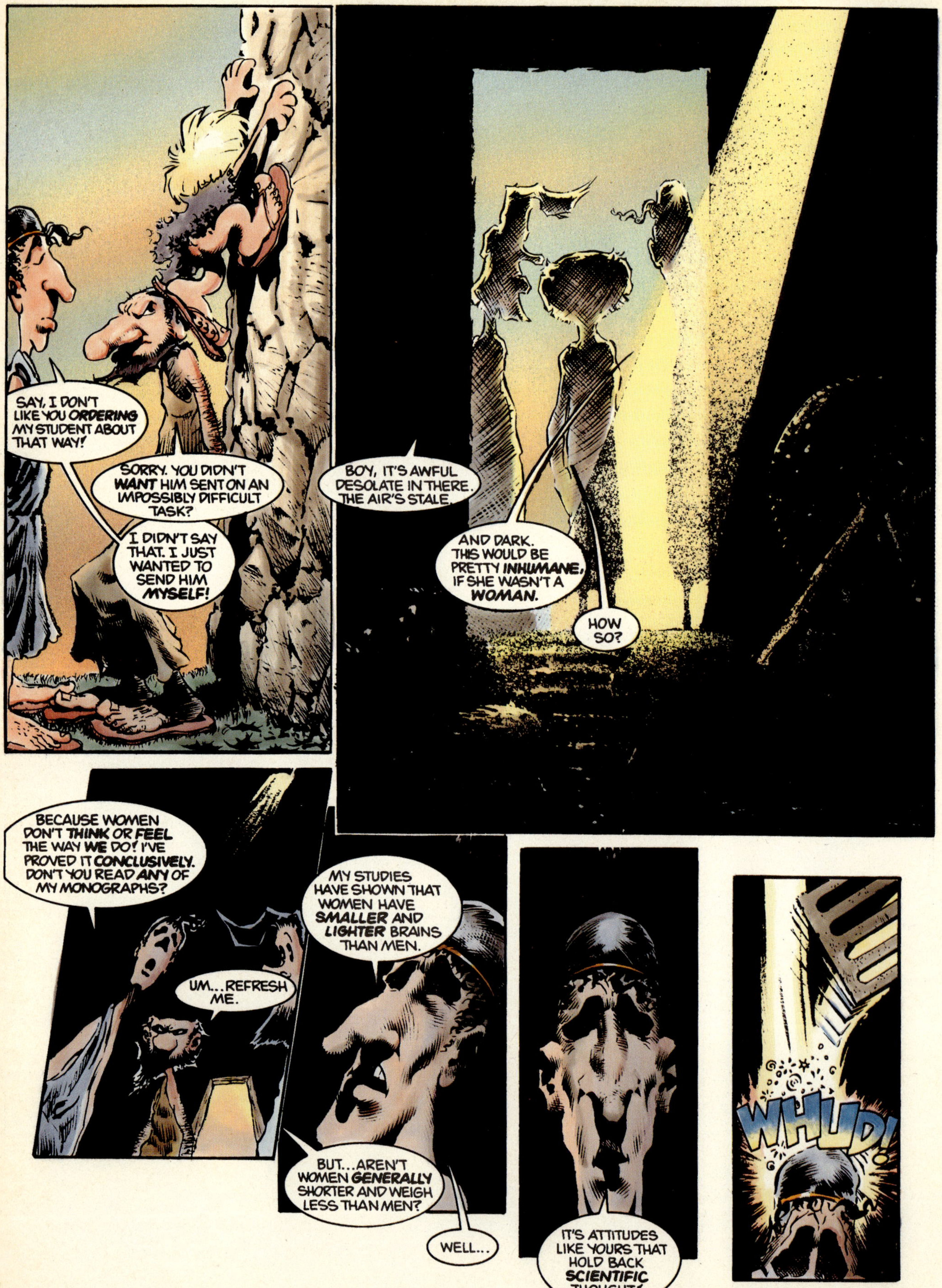
SAY, I DON'T LIKE YOU ORDERING MY STUDENT ABOUT THAT WAY!
SORRY. YOU DIDN'T WANT HIM SENT ON AN IMPOSSIBLY DIFFICULT TASK?
I DIDN'T SAY THAT. I JUST WANTED TO SEND HIM MYSELF!
BOY, IT'S AWFUL DESOLATE IN THERE. THE AIR'S STALE.
AND DARK. THIS WOULD BE PRETTY INHUMANE, IF SHE WASN'T A WOMAN.
HOW SO?
BECAUSE WOMEN DON'T THINK OR FEEL THE WAY WE DO! I'VE PROVED IT CONCLUSIVELY. DON'T YOU READ ANY OF MY MONOGRAPHS?
UM...REFRESH ME.
MY STUDIES HAVE SHOWN THAT WOMEN HAVE SMALLER AND LIGHTER BRAINS THAN MEN.
BUT...AREN'T WOMEN GENERALLY SHORTER AND WEIGH LESS THAN MEN?
WELL...
IT'S ATTITUDES LIKE YOURS THAT HOLD BACK SCIENTIFIC THOUGHT!
WHUD!

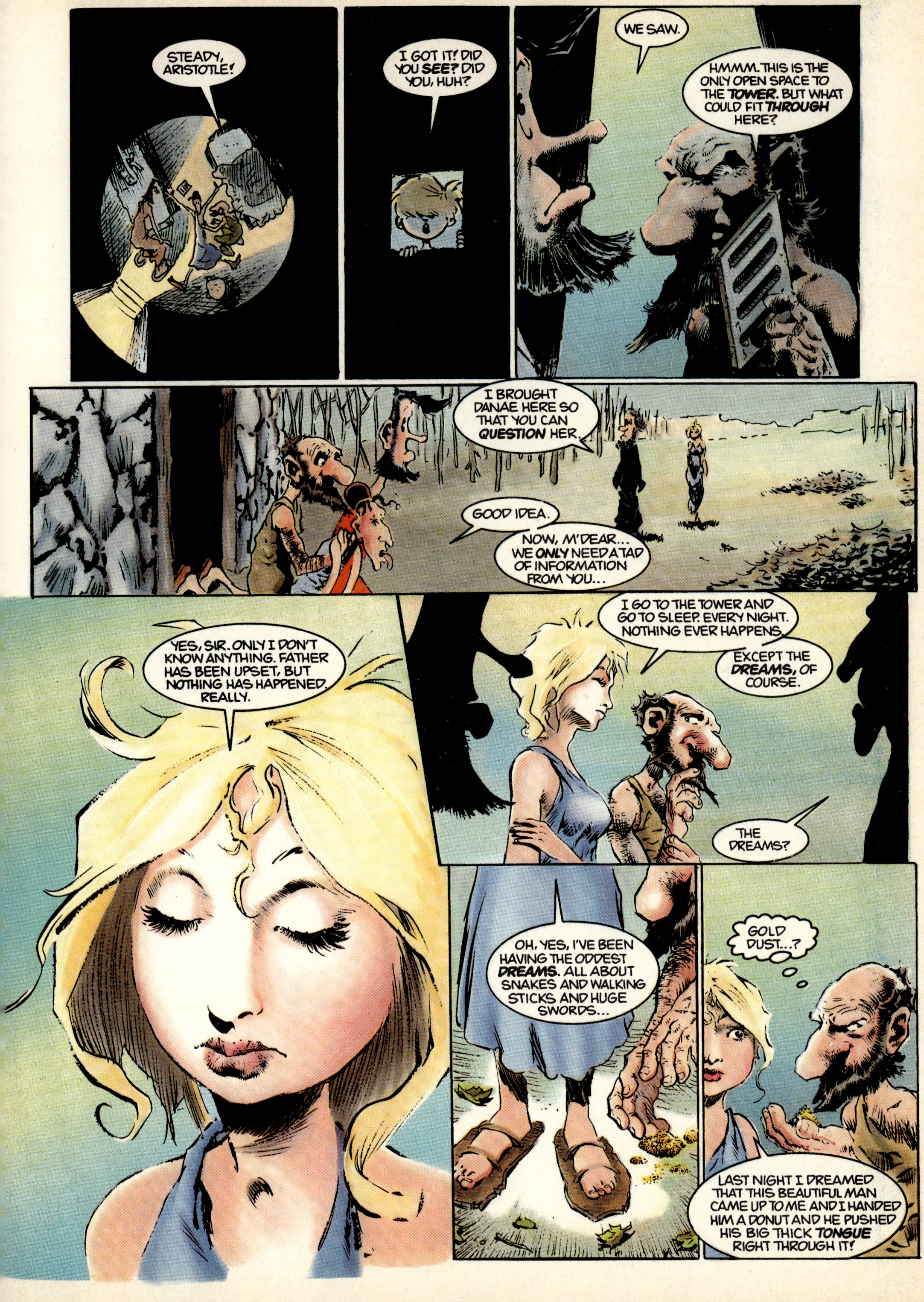
STEADY, ARISTOTLE!
I GOT IT! DID YOU SEE? DID YOU, HUH?
WE SAW.
HMMM. THIS IS THE ONLY OPEN SPACE TO THE TOWER. BUT WHAT COULD FIT THROUGH HERE?
I BROUGHT DANAE HERE SO THAT YOU CAN QUESTION HER.
GOOD IDEA.
NOW, M'DEAR... WE ONLY NEED A TAD OF INFORMATION FROM YOU...
YES, SIR. ONLY I DON'T KNOW ANYTHING. FATHER HAS BEEN UPSET, BUT NOTHING HAS HAPPENED. REALLY.
I GO TO THE TOWER AND GO TO SLEEP. EVERY NIGHT. NOTHING EVER HAPPENS.
EXCEPT THE DREAMS, OF COURSE.
THE DREAMS?
OH, YES, I'VE BEEN HAVING THE ODDEST DREAMS. ALL ABOUT SNAKES AND WALKING STICKS AND HUGE SWORDS...
GOLD DUST...?
LAST NIGHT I DREAMED THAT THIS BEAUTIFUL MAN CAME UP TO ME AND I HANDED HIM A DONUT AND HE PUSHED HIS BIG THICK TONGUE RIGHT THROUGH IT!

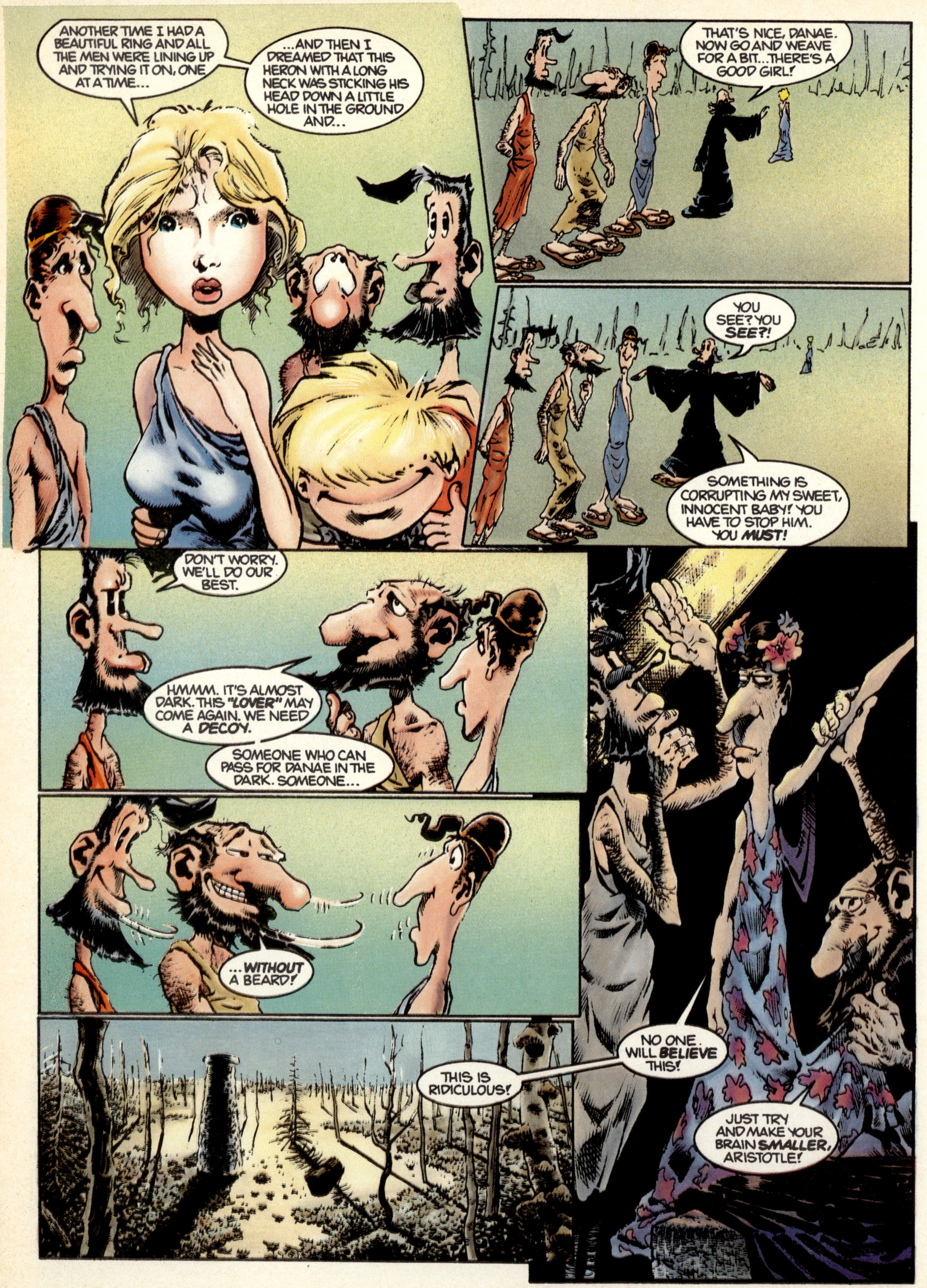
ANOTHER TIME I HAD A BEAUTIFUL RING AND ALL THE MEN WERE LINING UP AND TRYING IT ON, ONE AT A TIME...
...AND THEN I DREAMED THAT THIS HERON WITH A LONG NECK WAS STICKING HIS HEAD DOWN A LITTLE HOLE IN THE GROUND AND...
THAT'S NICE, DANAE. NOW GO AND WEAVE FOR A BIT... THERE'S A GOOD GIRL!
YOU SEE? YOU SEE?!
SOMETHING IS CORRUPTING MY SWEET, INNOCENT BABY! YOU HAVE TO STOP HIM. YOU MUST!
DON'T WORRY. WE'LL DO OUR BEST.
HMMM. IT'S ALMOST DARK. THIS "LOVER" MAY COME AGAIN. WE NEED A DECOY.
SOMEONE WHO CAN PASS FOR DANAE IN THE DARK. SOMEONE...
...WITHOUT A BEARD!
THIS IS RIDICULOUS!
NO ONE. WILL BELIEVE THIS!
JUST TRY AND MAKE YOUR BRAIN SMALLER, ARISTOTLE!

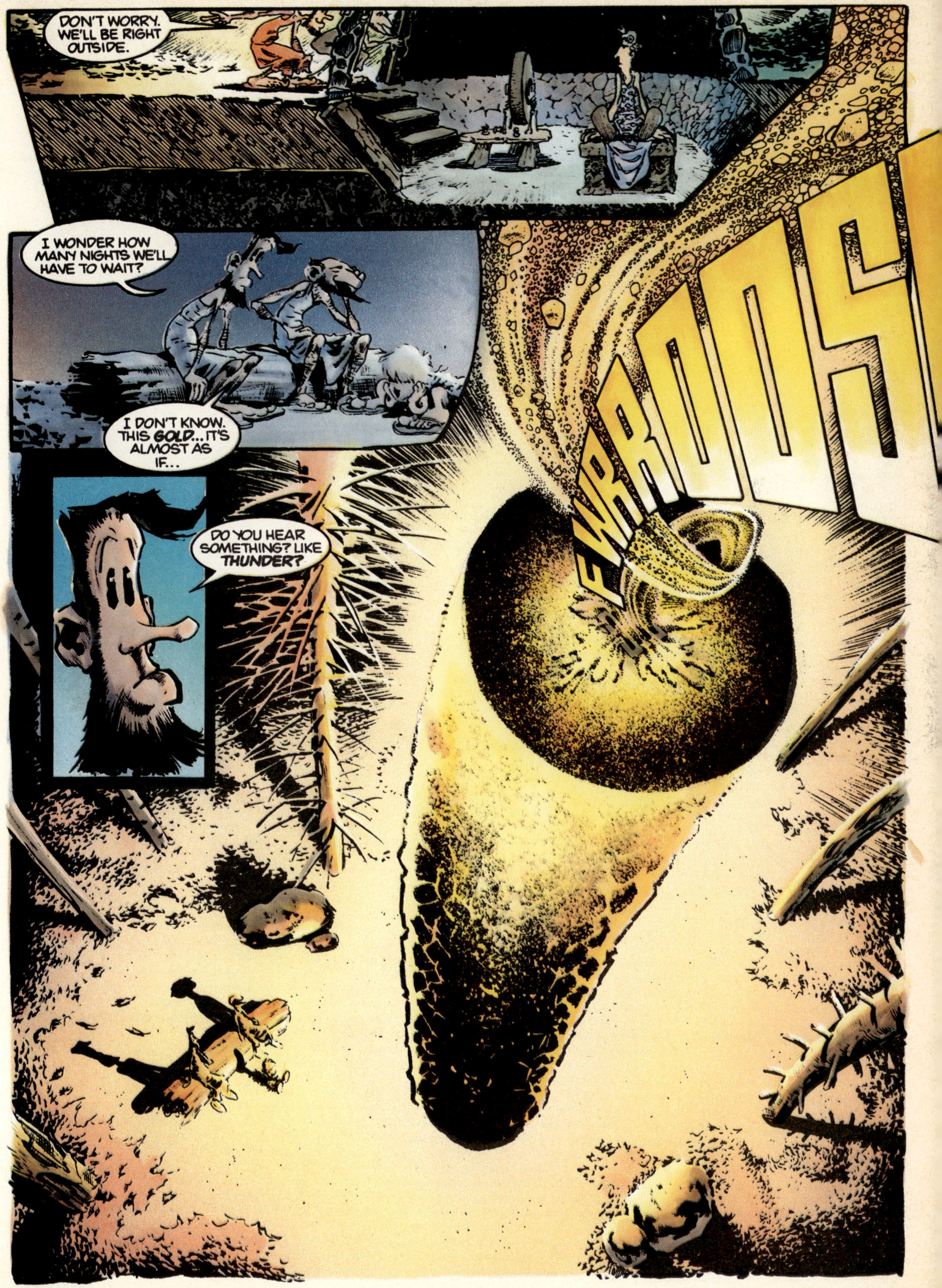
DON'T WORRY. WE'LL BE RIGHT OUTSIDE.
I WONDER HOW MANY NIGHTS WE'LL HAVE TO WAIT?
I DON'T KNOW. THIS GOLD... IT'S ALMOST AS IF...
DO YOU HEAR SOMETHING? LIKE THUNDER?
FWRROOSH

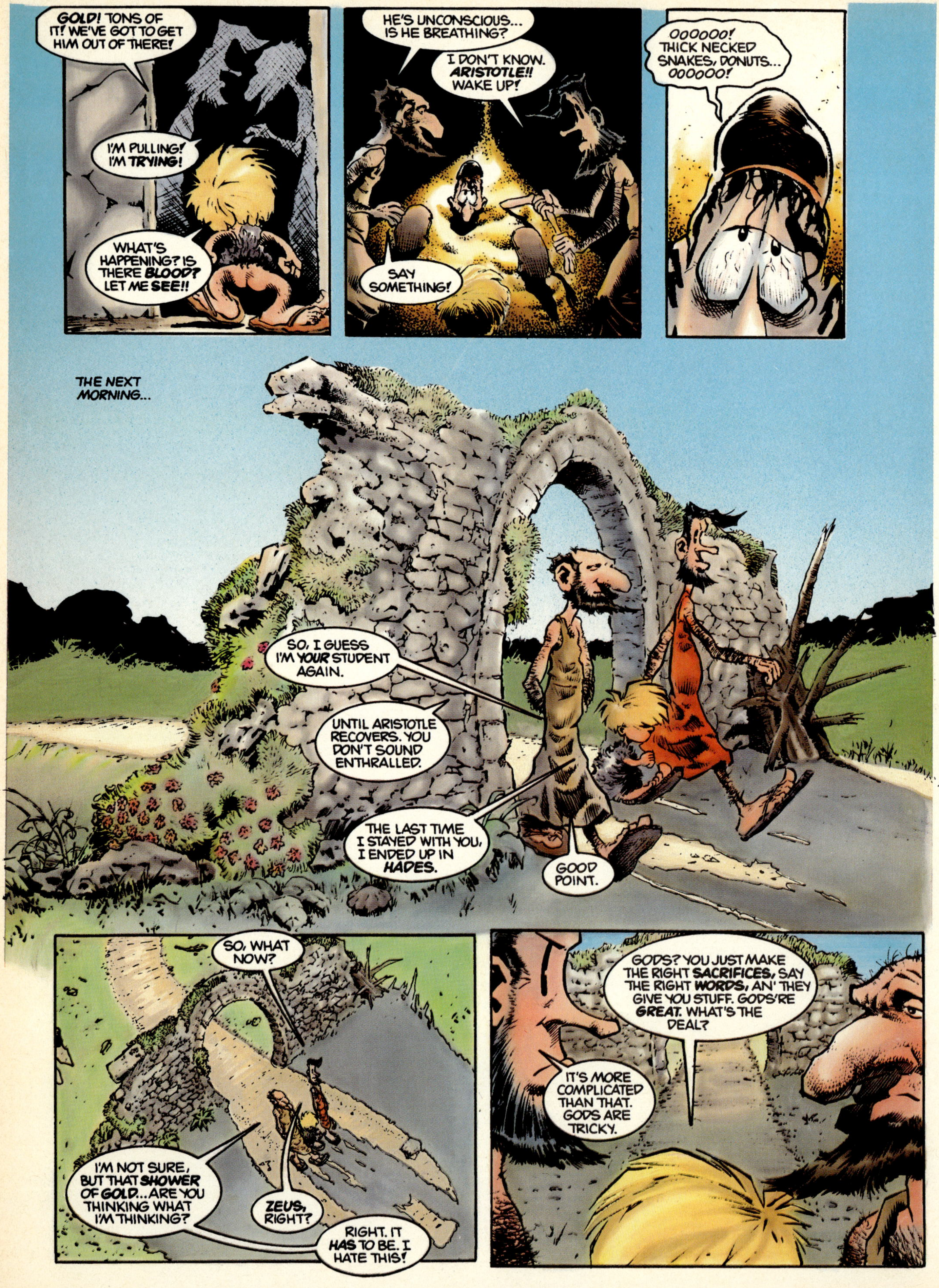

GOLD! TONS OF IT! WE'VE GOT TO GET HIM OUT OF THERE!
I'M PULLING! I'M TRYING!
WHAT'S HAPPENING? IS THERE BLOOD? LET ME SEE!!
HE'S UNCONSCIOUS... IS HE BREATHING?
I DON'T KNOW. ARISTOTLE!! WAKE UP!
SAY SOMETHING!
OOOOOO! THICK NECKED SNAKES, DONUTS... OOOOOO!
THE NEXT MORNING...
SO, I GUESS I'M YOUR STUDENT AGAIN.
UNTIL ARISTOTLE RECOVERS. YOU DON'T SOUND ENTHRALLED.
THE LAST TIME I STAYED WITH YOU, I ENDED UP IN HADES.
GOOD POINT.
SO, WHAT NOW?
I'M NOT SURE, BUT THAT SHOWER OF GOLD... ARE YOU THINKING WHAT I'M THINKING?
ZEUS, RIGHT?
RIGHT. IT HAS TO BE. I HATE THIS!
GODS? YOU JUST MAKE THE RIGHT SACRIFICES, SAY THE RIGHT WORDS, AN' THEY GIVE YOU STUFF. GODS'RE GREAT. WHAT'S THE DEAL?
IT'S MORE COMPLICATED THAN THAT. GODS ARE TRICKY.

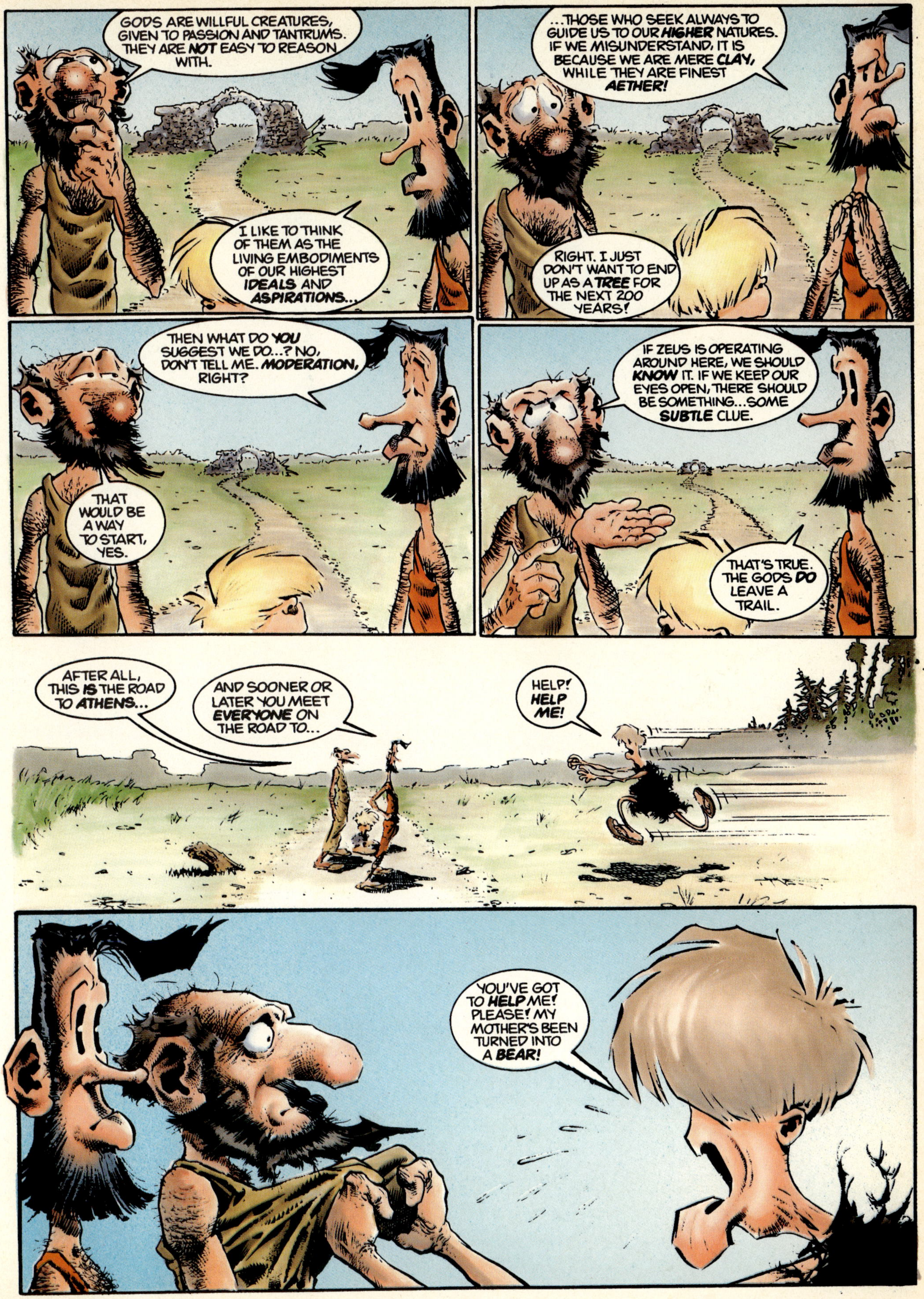

GODS ARE WILLFUL CREATURES, GIVEN TO PASSION AND TANTRUMS. THEY ARE NOT EASY TO REASON WITH.
I LIKE TO THINK OF THEM AS THE LIVING EMBODIMENTS OF OUR HIGHEST IDEALS AND ASPIRATIONS...
...THOSE WHO SEEK ALWAYS TO GUIDE US TO OUR HIGHER NATURES. IF WE MISUNDERSTAND, IT IS BECAUSE WE ARE MERE CLAY, WHILE THEY ARE FINEST AETHER!
RIGHT. I JUST DON'T WANT TO END UP AS A TREE FOR THE NEXT 200 YEARS!
THEN WHAT DO YOU SUGGEST WE DO...? NO, DON'T TELL ME. MODERATION, RIGHT?
THAT WOULD BE A WAY TO START, YES.
IF ZEUS IS OPERATING AROUND HERE, WE SHOULD KNOW IT. IF WE KEEP OUR EYES OPEN, THERE SHOULD BE SOMETHING...SOME SUBTLE CLUE.
THAT'S TRUE. THE GODS DO LEAVE A TRAIL.
AFTER ALL, THIS IS THE ROAD TO ATHENS...
AND SOONER OR LATER YOU MEET EVERYONE ON THE ROAD TO...
HELP! HELP ME!
YOU'VE GOT TO HELP ME! PLEASE! MY MOTHER'S BEEN TURNED INTO A BEAR!

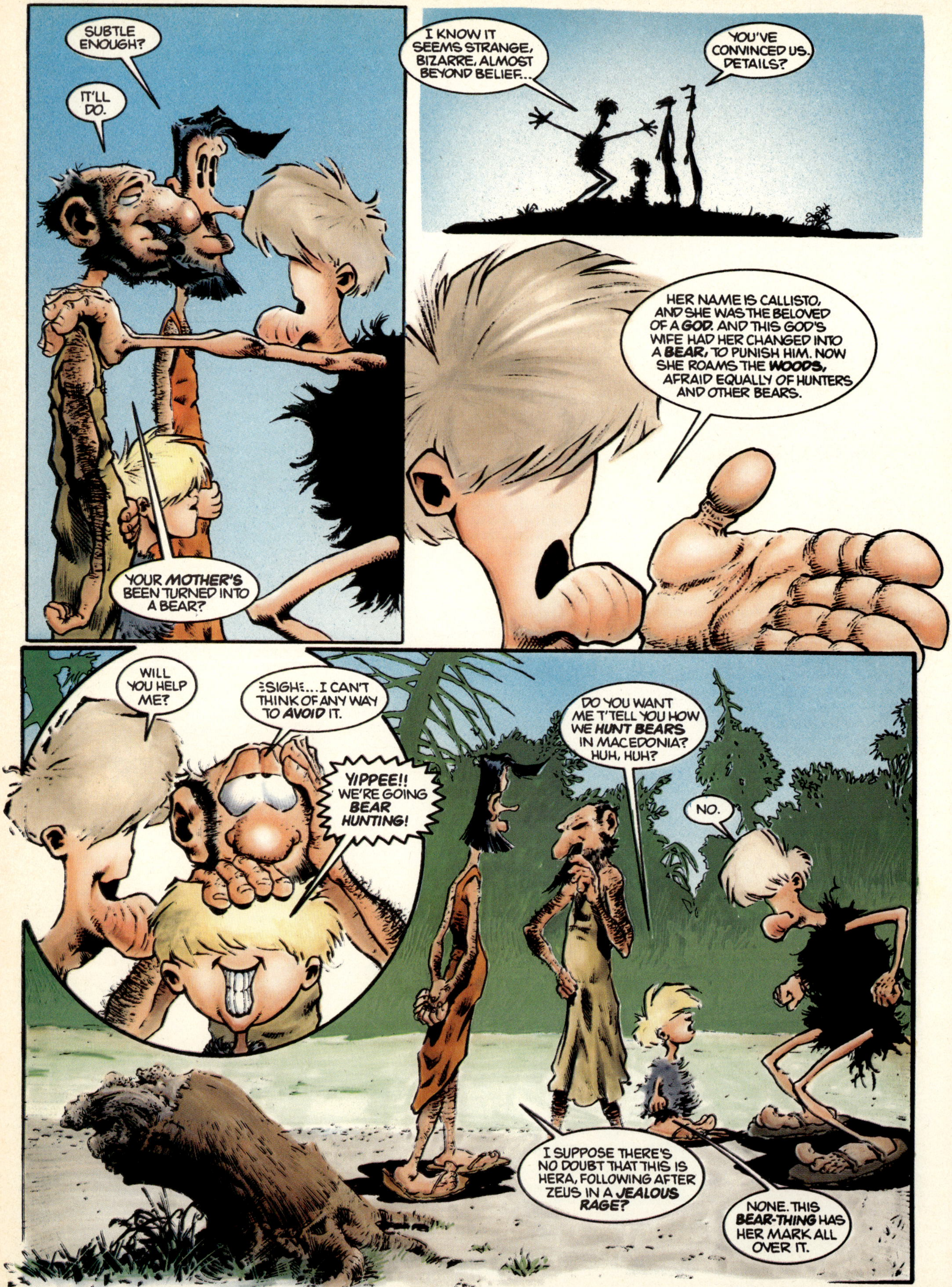

SUBTLE ENOUGH?
IT'LL DO.
YOUR MOTHER'S BEEN TURNED INTO A BEAR?
I KNOW IT SEEMS STRANGE, BIZARRE, ALMOST BEYOND BELIEF...
YOU'VE CONVINCED US. DETAILS?
HER NAME IS CALLISTO, AND SHE WAS THE BELOVED OF A GOD. AND THIS GOD'S WIFE HAD HER CHANGED INTO A BEAR, TO PUNISH HIM. NOW SHE ROAMS THE WOODS, AFRAID EQUALLY OF HUNTERS AND OTHER BEARS.
WILL YOU HELP ME?
SIGH... I CAN'T THINK OF ANY WAY TO AVOID IT.
YIPPEE!! WE'RE GOING BEAR HUNTING!
DO YOU WANT ME T'TELL YOU HOW WE HUNT BEARS IN MACEDONIA? HUH, HUH?
NO.
I SUPPOSE THERE'S NO DOUBT THAT THIS IS HERA, FOLLOWING AFTER ZEUS IN A JEALOUS RAGE?
NONE. THIS BEAR-THING HAS HER MARK ALL OVER IT.

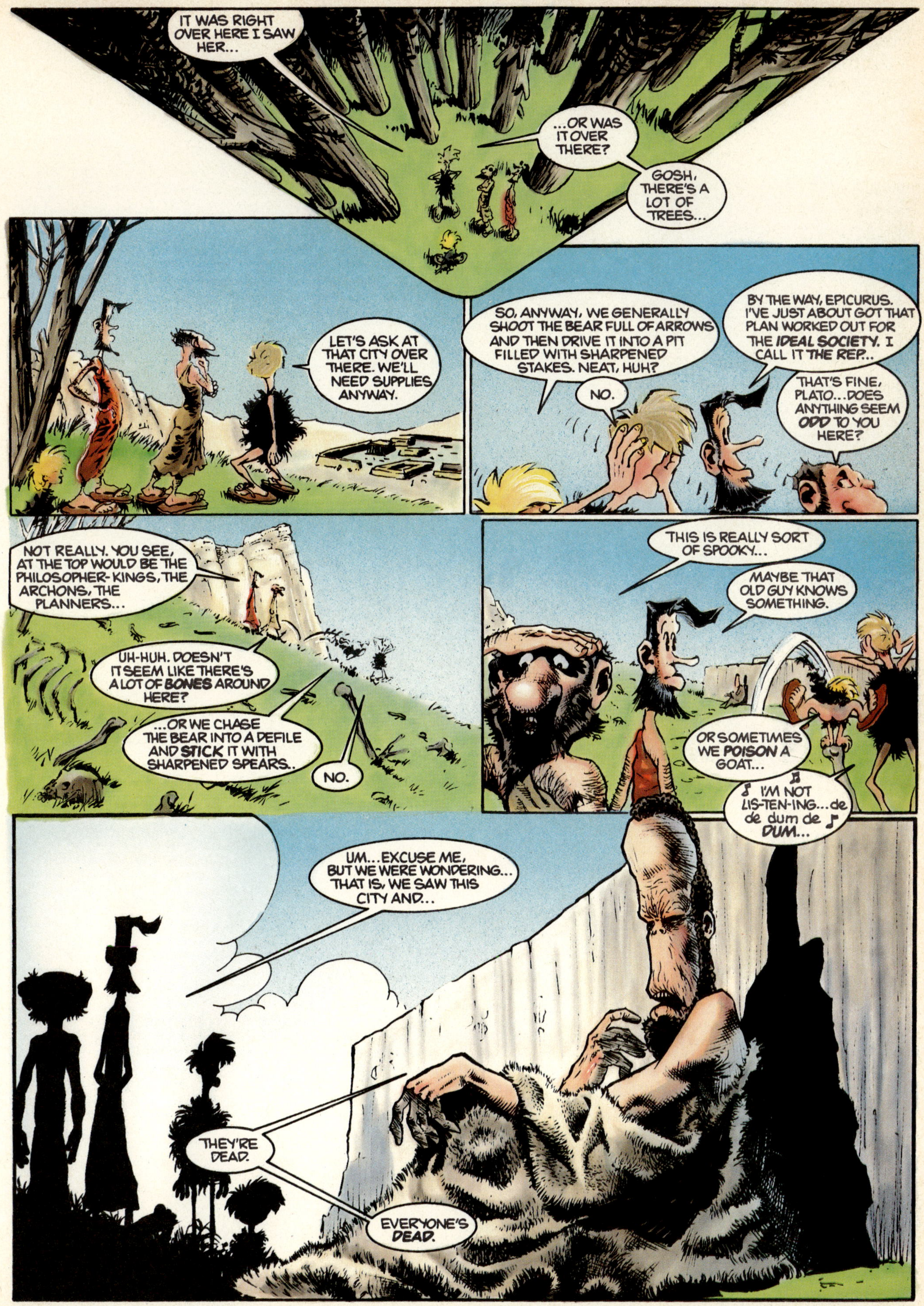

IT WAS RIGHT OVER HERE I SAW HER...
...OR WAS IT OVER THERE?
GOSH, THERE'S A LOT OF TREES...
LET'S ASK AT THAT CITY OVER THERE. WE'LL NEED SUPPLIES ANYWAY.
SO, ANYWAY, WE GENERALLY SHOOT THE BEAR FULL OF ARROWS AND THEN DRIVE IT INTO A PIT FILLED WITH SHARPENED STAKES. NEAT, HUH?
NO.
BY THE WAY, EPICURUS. I'VE JUST ABOUT GOT THAT PLAN WORKED OUT FOR THE **IDEAL SOCIETY.** I CALL IT **THE REP**...
THAT'S FINE, PLATO...DOES ANYTHING SEEM **ODD** TO YOU HERE?
NOT REALLY. YOU SEE, AT THE TOP WOULD BE THE PHILOSOPHER-KINGS, THE ARCHONS, THE PLANNERS...
UH-HUH. DOESN'T IT SEEM LIKE THERE'S A LOT OF **BONES** AROUND HERE?
...OR WE CHASE THE BEAR INTO A DEFILE AND **STICK** IT WITH SHARPENED SPEARS.
NO.
THIS IS REALLY SORT OF SPOOKY...
MAYBE THAT OLD GUY KNOWS SOMETHING.
OR SOMETIMES WE **POISON** A GOAT...
♪ I'M NOT LIS-TEN-ING...de de dum de **DUM**... ♪
UM...EXCUSE ME, BUT WE WERE WONDERING... THAT IS, WE SAW THIS CITY AND...
THEY'RE DEAD.
EVERYONE'S **DEAD**.

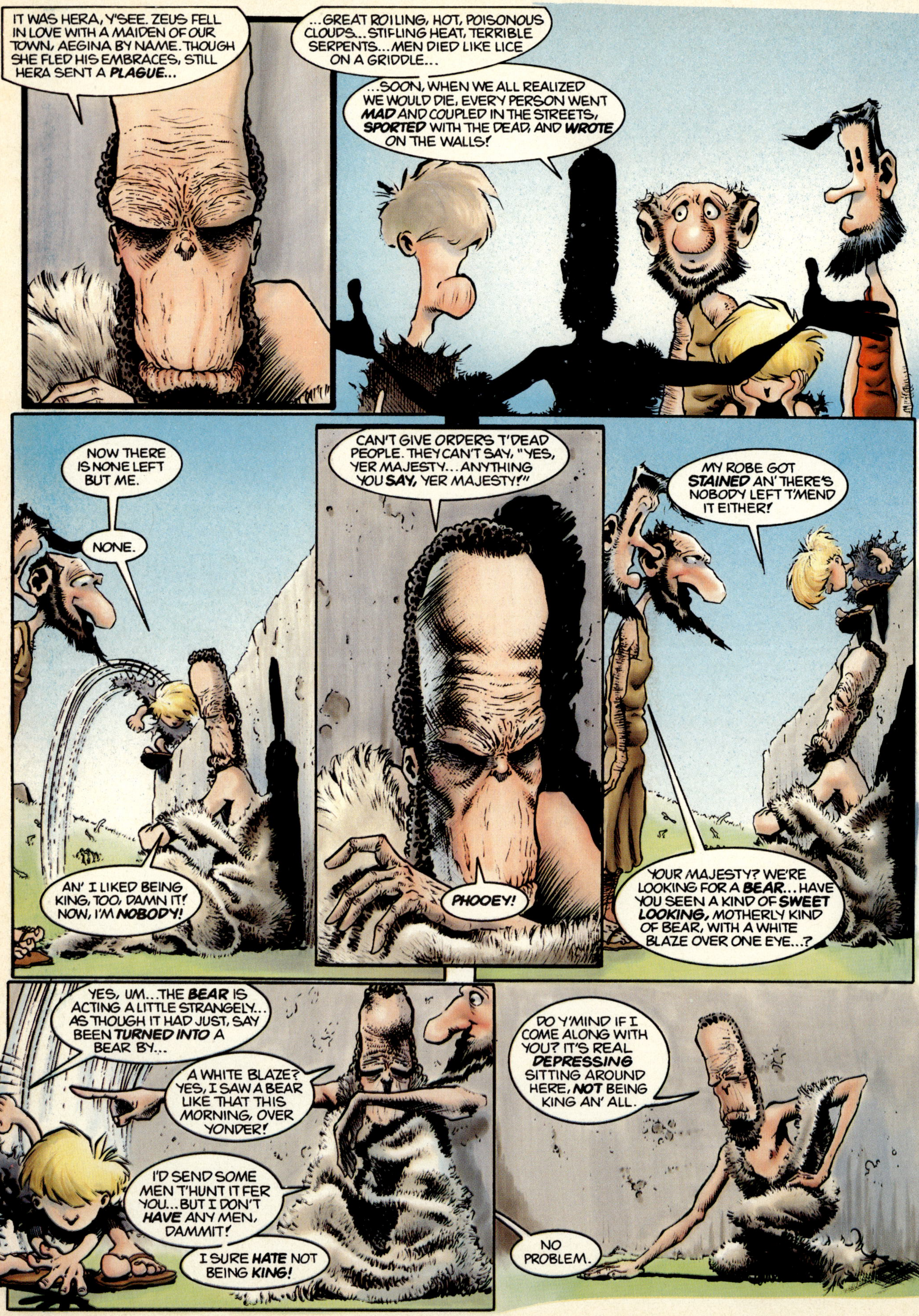

IT WAS HERA, Y'SEE. ZEUS FELL IN LOVE WITH A MAIDEN OF OUR TOWN, AEGINA BY NAME. THOUGH SHE FLED HIS EMBRACES, STILL HERA SENT A PLAGUE...
...GREAT ROILING, HOT, POISONOUS CLOUDS... STIFLING HEAT, TERRIBLE SERPENTS... MEN DIED LIKE LICE ON A GRIDDLE...
...SOON, WHEN WE ALL REALIZED WE WOULD DIE, EVERY PERSON WENT MAD AND COUPLED IN THE STREETS, SPORTED WITH THE DEAD, AND WROTE ON THE WALLS!
NOW THERE IS NONE LEFT BUT ME.
NONE.
AN' I LIKED BEING KING, TOO, DAMN IT! NOW, I'M NOBODY!
CAN'T GIVE ORDERS T'DEAD PEOPLE. THEY CAN'T SAY, "YES, YER MAJESTY... ANYTHING YOU SAY, YER MAJESTY!"
PHOOEY!
MY ROBE GOT STAINED AN' THERE'S NOBODY LEFT T'MEND IT EITHER!
YOUR MAJESTY? WE'RE LOOKING FOR A BEAR... HAVE YOU SEEN A KIND OF SWEET LOOKING, MOTHERLY KIND OF BEAR, WITH A WHITE BLAZE OVER ONE EYE...?
YES, UM... THE BEAR IS ACTING A LITTLE STRANGELY... AS THOUGH IT HAD JUST, SAY BEEN TURNED INTO A BEAR BY...
A WHITE BLAZE? YES, I SAW A BEAR LIKE THAT THIS MORNING, OVER YONDER!
I'D SEND SOME MEN T'HUNT IT FER YOU... BUT I DON'T HAVE ANY MEN, DAMMIT!
I SURE HATE NOT BEING KING!
DO Y'MIND IF I COME ALONG WITH YOU? IT'S REAL DEPRESSING SITTING AROUND HERE, NOT BEING KING AN' ALL.
NO PROBLEM.

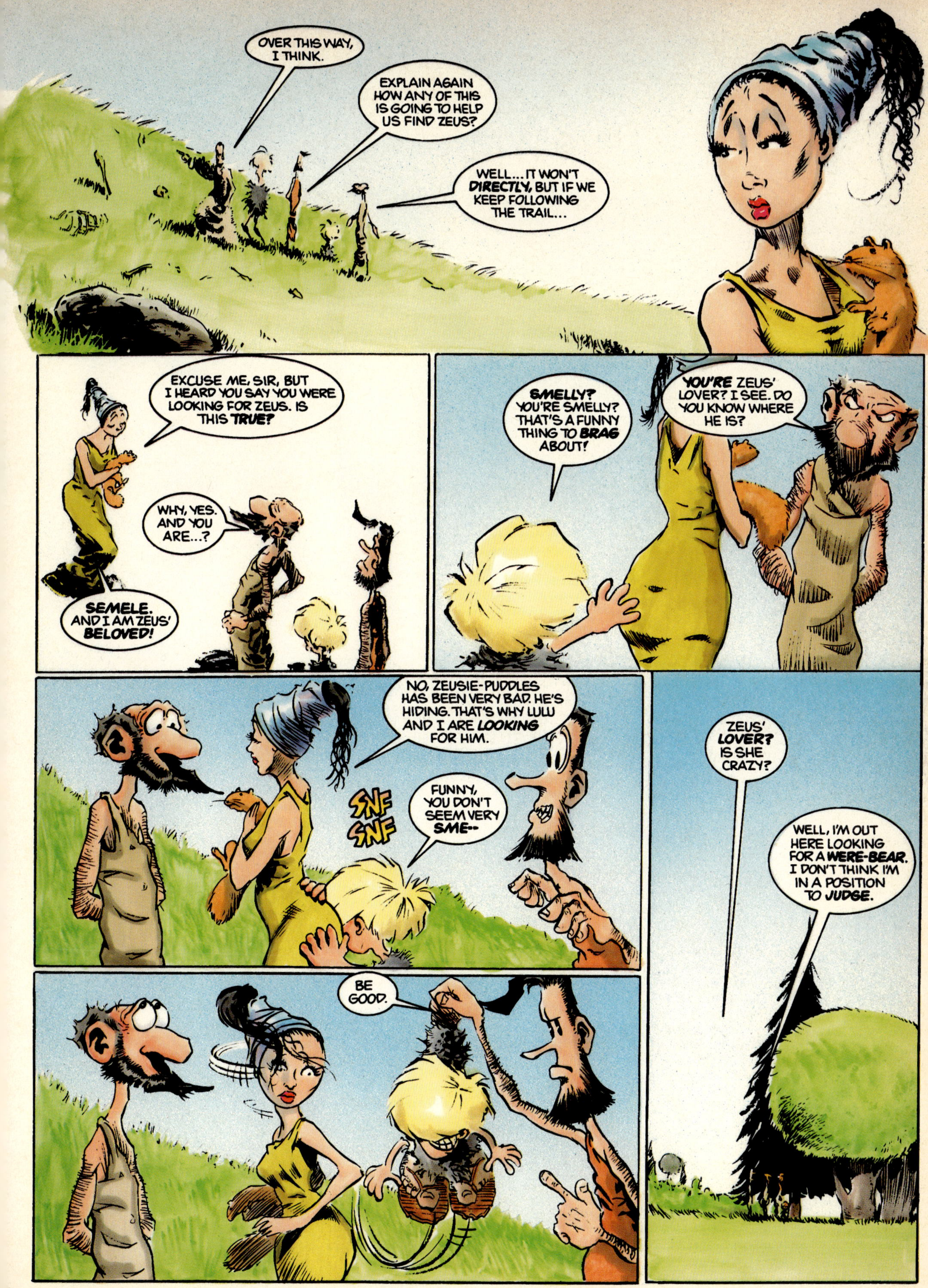
OVER THIS WAY, I THINK.
EXPLAIN AGAIN HOW ANY OF THIS IS GOING TO HELP US FIND ZEUS?
WELL... IT WON'T DIRECTLY, BUT IF WE KEEP FOLLOWING THE TRAIL...
EXCUSE ME, SIR, BUT I HEARD YOU SAY YOU WERE LOOKING FOR ZEUS. IS THIS TRUE?
WHY, YES. AND YOU ARE...?
SEMELE. AND I AM ZEUS' BELOVED!
YOU'RE ZEUS' LOVER? I SEE. DO YOU KNOW WHERE HE IS?
SMELLY? YOU'RE SMELLY? THAT'S A FUNNY THING TO BRAG ABOUT!
NO, ZEUSIE-PUDDLES HAS BEEN VERY BAD. HE'S HIDING. THAT'S WHY LULU AND I ARE LOOKING FOR HIM.
SNF SNF
FUNNY, YOU DON'T SEEM VERY SME--
BE GOOD.
ZEUS' LOVER? IS SHE CRAZY?
WELL, I'M OUT HERE LOOKING FOR A WERE-BEAR. I DON'T THINK I'M IN A POSITION TO JUDGE.

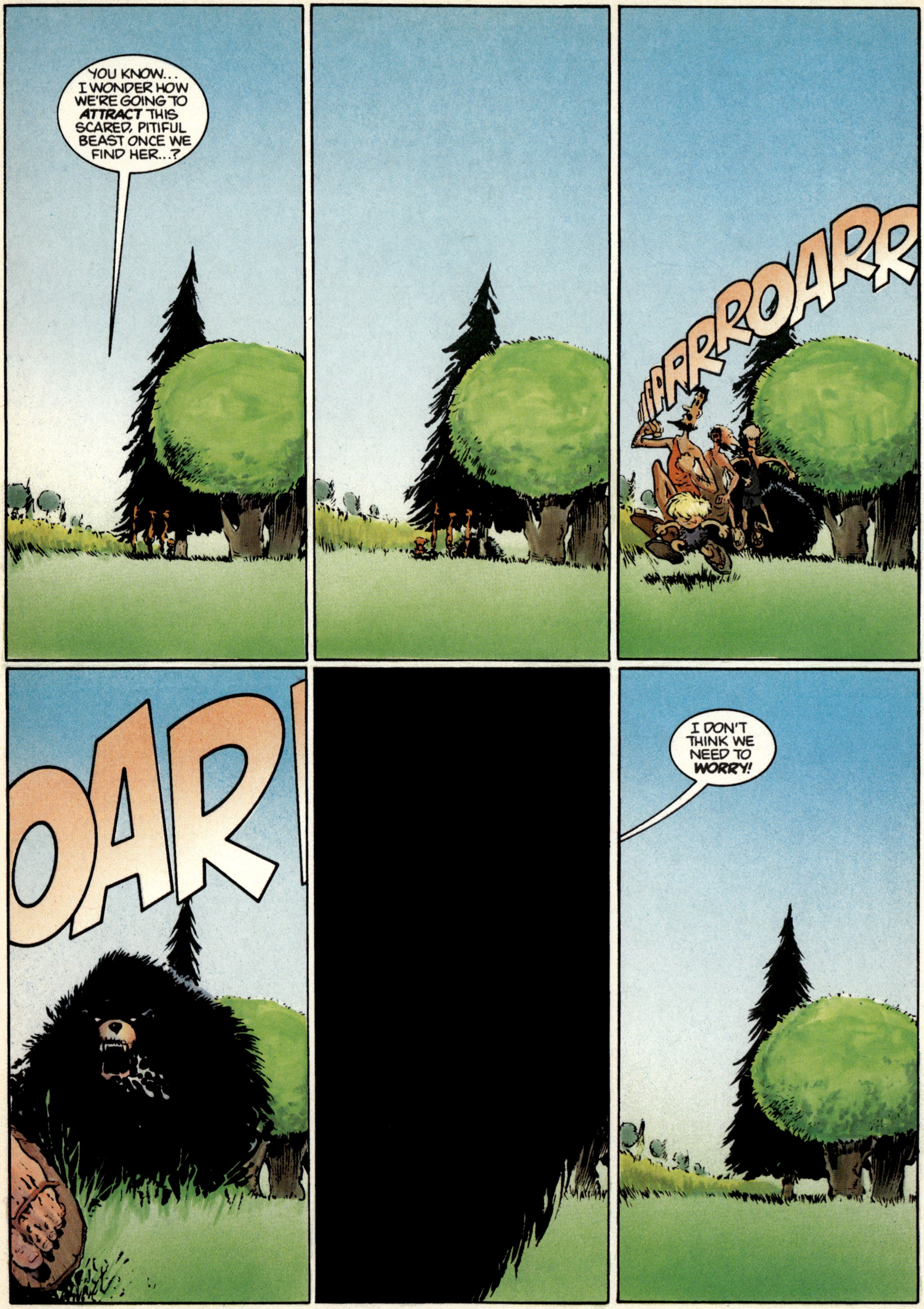
YOU KNOW... I WONDER HOW WE'RE GOING TO **ATTRACT** THIS SCARED, PITIFUL BEAST ONCE WE FIND HER...?
RRROARR
OAR
I DON'T THINK WE NEED TO **WORRY**!

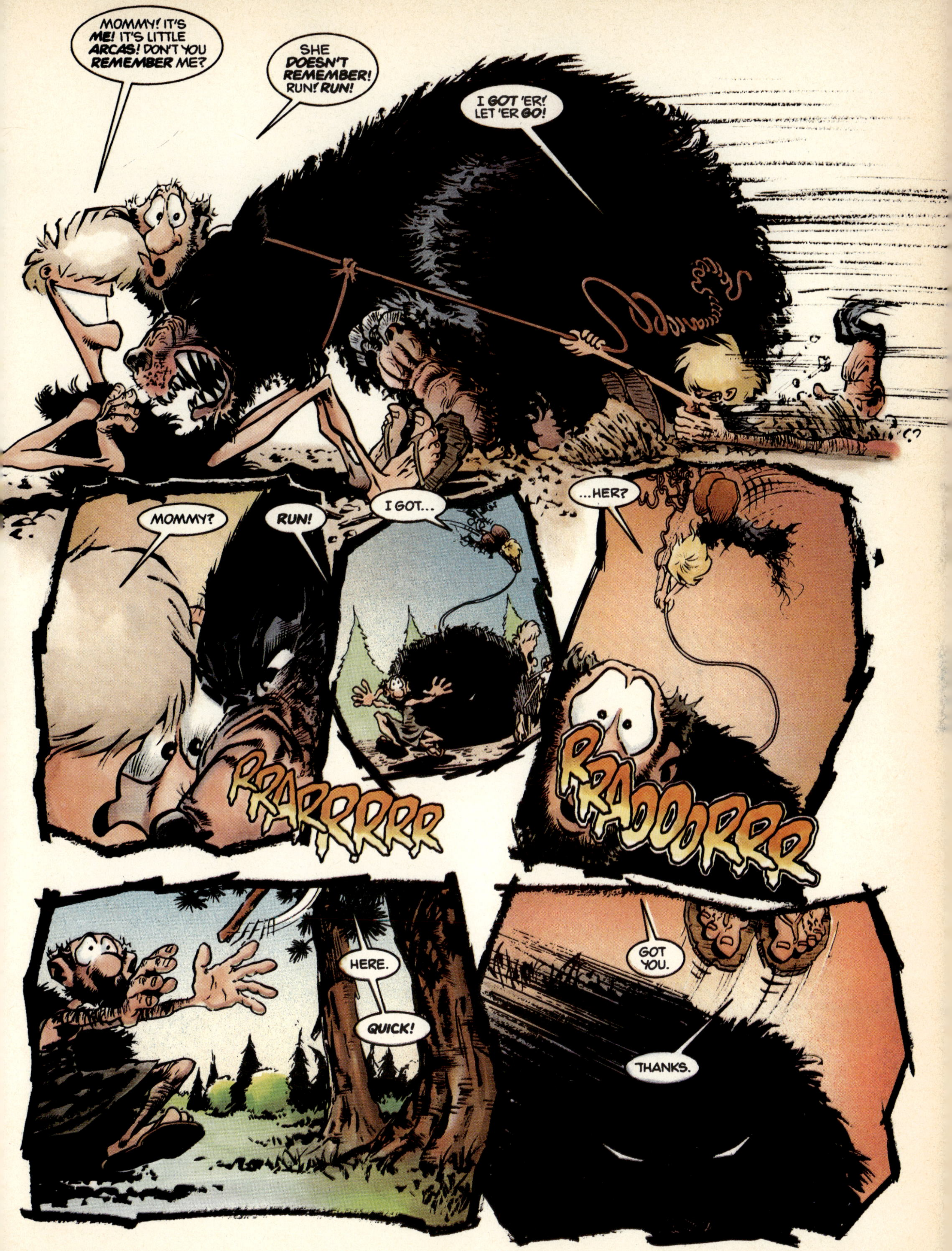
MOMMY! IT'S ME! IT'S LITTLE ARCAS! DON'T YOU REMEMBER ME?
SHE DOESN'T REMEMBER! RUN! RUN!
I GOT 'ER! LET 'ER GO!
MOMMY?
RUN!
I GOT...
...HER?
RRARRRRR
RRAOOORRR
HERE.
QUICK!
GOT YOU.
THANKS.

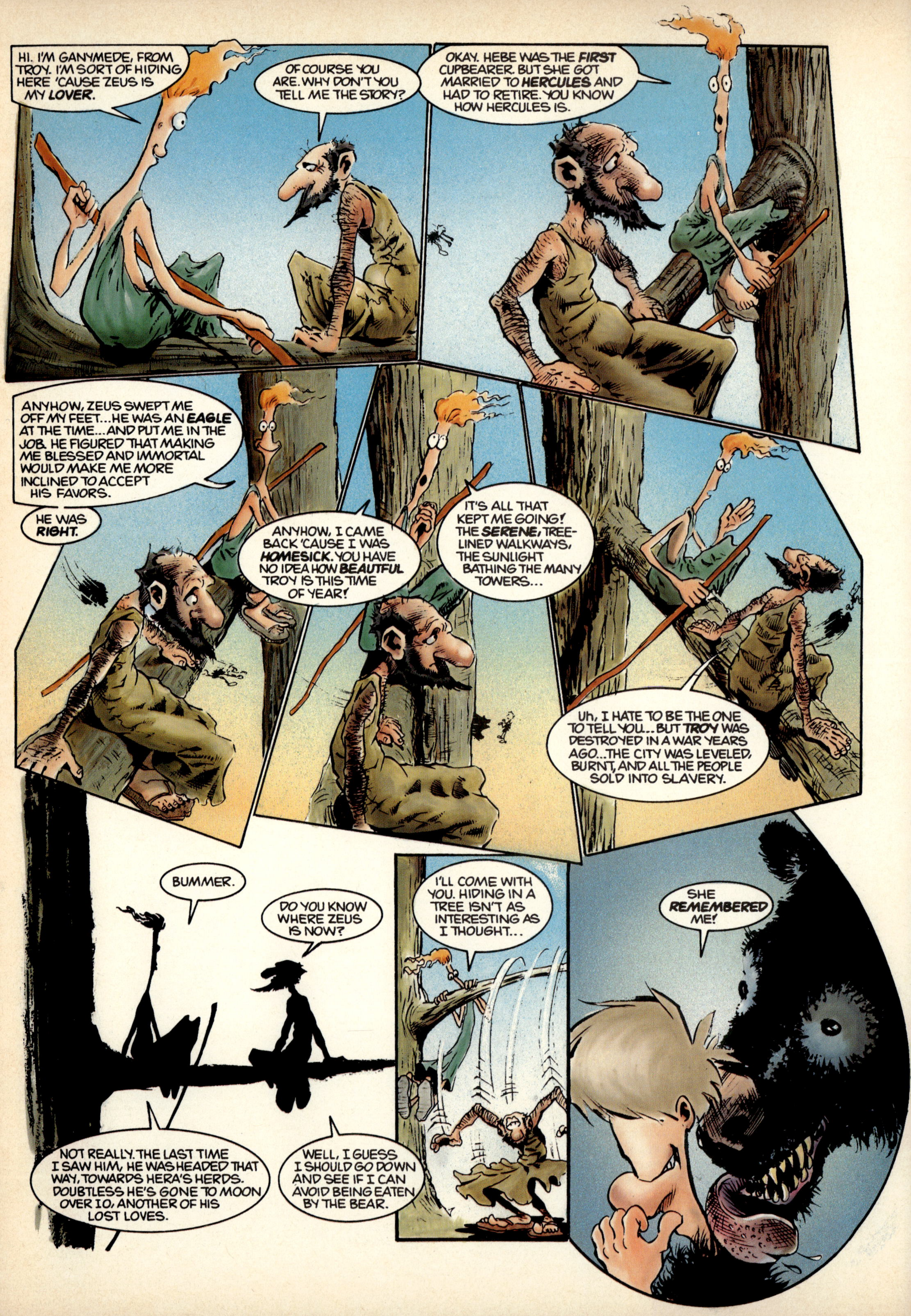
HI. I'M GANYMEDE, FROM TROY. I'M SORT OF HIDING HERE 'CAUSE ZEUS IS MY **LOVER**.
OF COURSE YOU ARE. WHY DON'T YOU TELL ME THE STORY?
OKAY. HEBE WAS THE **FIRST** CUPBEARER. BUT SHE GOT MARRIED TO **HERCULES** AND HAD TO RETIRE. YOU KNOW HOW HERCULES IS.
ANYHOW, ZEUS SWEPT ME OFF MY FEET...HE WAS AN **EAGLE** AT THE TIME...AND PUT ME IN THE JOB. HE FIGURED THAT MAKING ME BLESSED AND IMMORTAL WOULD MAKE ME MORE INCLINED TO ACCEPT HIS FAVORS.
HE WAS **RIGHT**.
ANYHOW, I CAME BACK 'CAUSE I WAS **HOMESICK**. YOU HAVE NO IDEA HOW **BEAUTFUL** TROY IS THIS TIME OF YEAR!
IT'S ALL THAT KEPT ME GOING! THE **SERENE**, TREE-LINED WALKWAYS, THE SUNLIGHT BATHING THE MANY TOWERS...
Uh, I HATE TO BE THE ONE TO TELL YOU... BUT **TROY** WAS DESTROYED IN A WAR YEARS AGO...THE CITY WAS LEVELED, BURNT, AND ALL THE PEOPLE SOLD INTO SLAVERY.
BUMMER.
DO YOU KNOW WHERE ZEUS IS NOW?
NOT REALLY. THE LAST TIME I SAW HIM, HE WAS HEADED THAT WAY, TOWARDS HERA'S HERDS. DOUBTLESS HE'S GONE TO MOON OVER IO, ANOTHER OF HIS LOST LOVES.
WELL, I GUESS I SHOULD GO DOWN AND SEE IF I CAN AVOID BEING EATEN BY THE BEAR.
I'LL COME WITH YOU. HIDING IN A TREE ISN'T AS INTERESTING AS I THOUGHT...
SHE **REMEMBERED** ME!

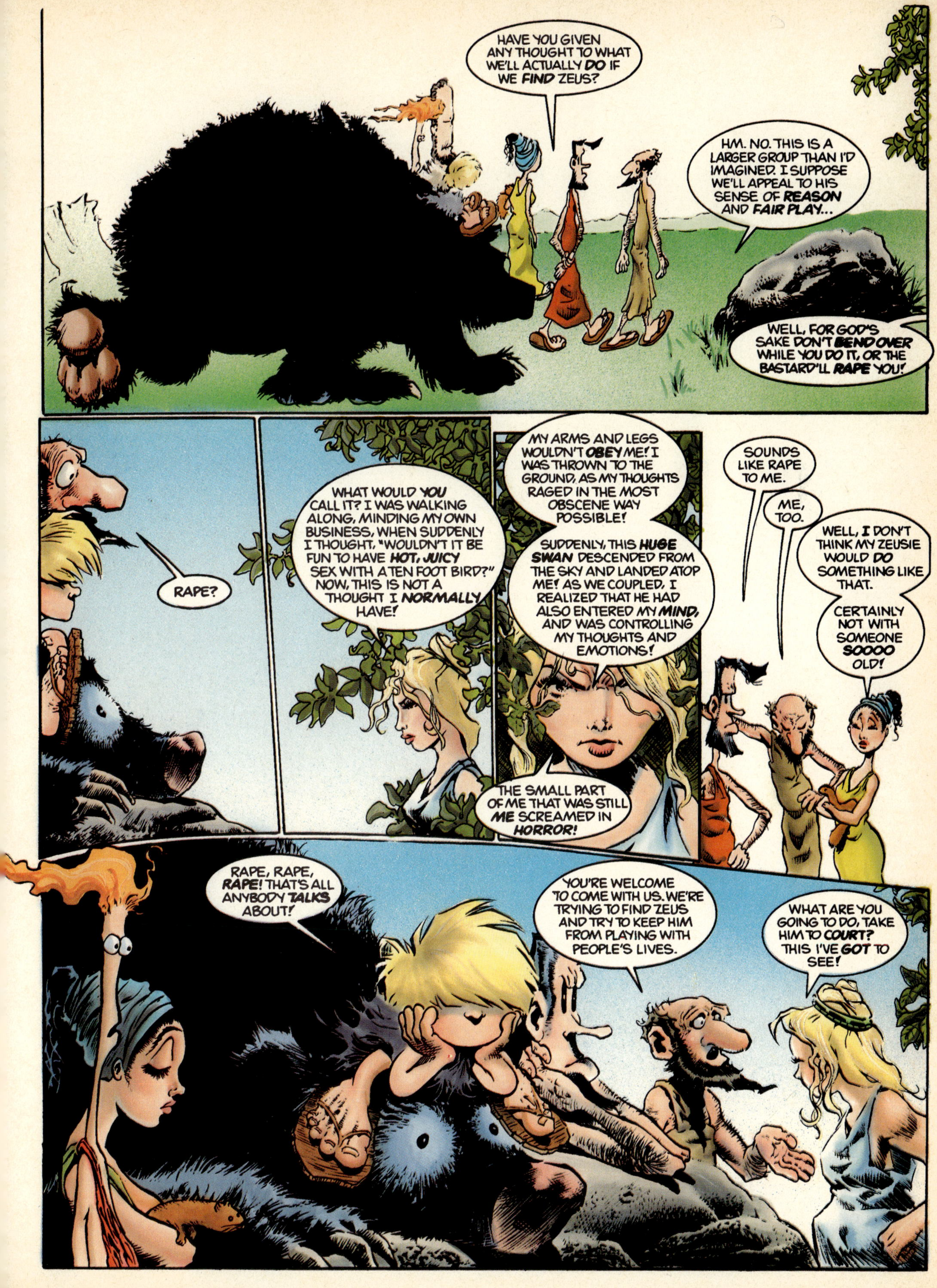
HAVE YOU GIVEN ANY THOUGHT TO WHAT WE'LL ACTUALLY **DO** IF WE **FIND** ZEUS?
HM. NO. THIS IS A LARGER GROUP THAN I'D IMAGINED. I SUPPOSE WE'LL APPEAL TO HIS SENSE OF **REASON** AND **FAIR PLAY...**
WELL, FOR GOD'S SAKE DON'T **BEND OVER** WHILE YOU DO IT, OR THE BASTARD'LL **RAPE** YOU!
RAPE?
WHAT WOULD **YOU** CALL IT? I WAS WALKING ALONG, MINDING MY OWN BUSINESS, WHEN SUDDENLY I THOUGHT, "WOULDN'T IT BE FUN TO HAVE **HOT, JUICY** SEX WITH A TEN FOOT BIRD?" NOW, THIS IS NOT A THOUGHT I **NORMALLY** HAVE!
MY ARMS AND LEGS WOULDN'T **OBEY** ME! I WAS THROWN TO THE GROUND, AS MY THOUGHTS RAGED IN THE MOST OBSCENE WAY POSSIBLE!
SUDDENLY, THIS **HUGE SWAN** DESCENDED FROM THE SKY AND LANDED ATOP ME! AS WE COUPLED, I REALIZED THAT HE HAD ALSO ENTERED MY **MIND**, AND WAS CONTROLLING MY THOUGHTS AND EMOTIONS!
THE SMALL PART OF ME THAT WAS STILL **ME** SCREAMED IN **HORROR!**
SOUNDS LIKE RAPE TO ME.
ME, TOO.
WELL, **I** DON'T THINK MY ZEUSIE WOULD **DO** SOMETHING LIKE THAT.
CERTAINLY NOT WITH SOMEONE **SOOOO** OLD!
RAPE, RAPE, **RAPE!** THAT'S ALL ANYBODY **TALKS** ABOUT!
YOU'RE WELCOME TO COME WITH US. WE'RE TRYING TO FIND ZEUS AND TRY TO KEEP HIM FROM PLAYING WITH PEOPLE'S LIVES.
WHAT ARE YOU GOING TO DO, TAKE HIM TO **COURT?** THIS I'VE **GOT** TO SEE!

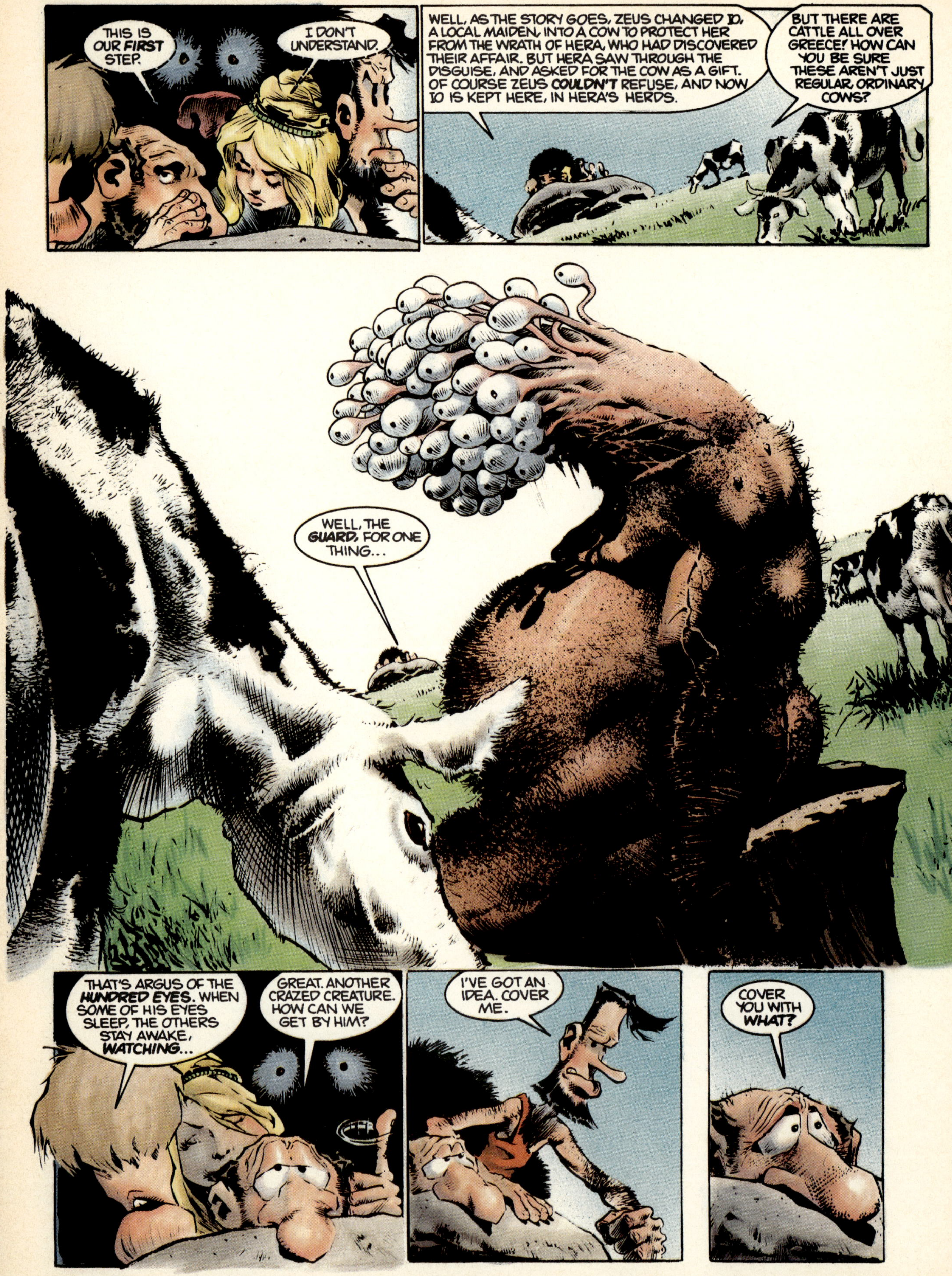
THIS IS OUR **FIRST** STEP.
I DON'T UNDERSTAND.
WELL, AS THE STORY GOES, ZEUS CHANGED IO, A LOCAL MAIDEN, INTO A COW TO PROTECT HER FROM THE WRATH OF HERA, WHO HAD DISCOVERED THEIR AFFAIR. BUT HERA SAW THROUGH THE DISGUISE, AND ASKED FOR THE COW AS A GIFT. OF COURSE ZEUS **COULDN'T** REFUSE, AND NOW IO IS KEPT HERE, IN HERA'S HERDS.
BUT THERE ARE CATTLE ALL OVER GREECE! HOW CAN YOU BE SURE THESE AREN'T JUST REGULAR, ORDINARY COWS?
WELL, THE **GUARD**, FOR ONE THING...
THAT'S ARGUS OF THE **HUNDRED EYES**. WHEN SOME OF HIS EYES SLEEP, THE OTHERS STAY AWAKE, **WATCHING**...
GREAT. ANOTHER CRAZED CREATURE. HOW CAN WE GET BY HIM?
I'VE GOT AN IDEA. COVER ME.
COVER YOU WITH **WHAT?**

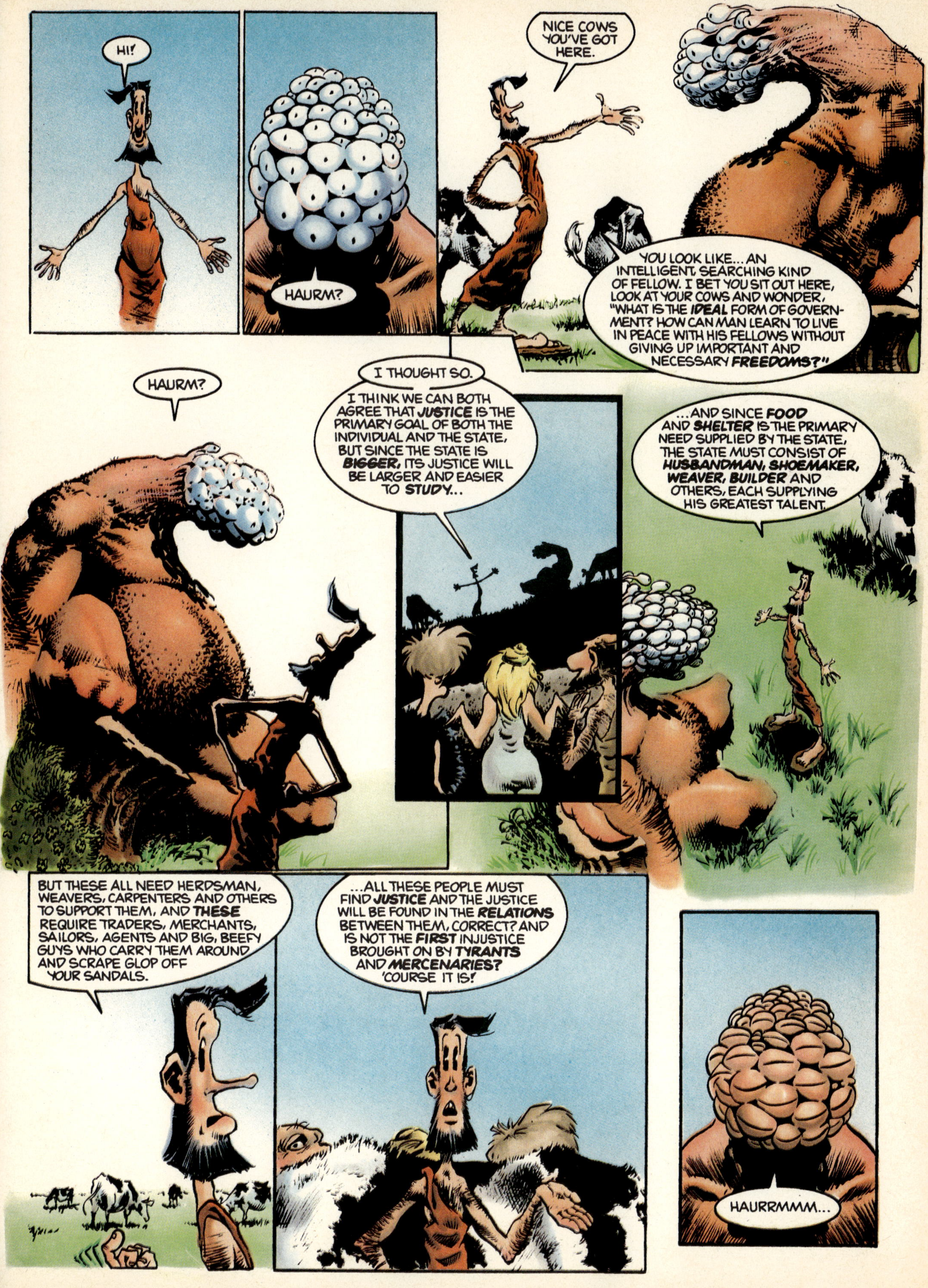

HI!
HAURM?
NICE COWS YOU'VE GOT HERE.
YOU LOOK LIKE... AN INTELLIGENT, SEARCHING KIND OF FELLOW. I BET YOU SIT OUT HERE, LOOK AT YOUR COWS AND WONDER, "WHAT IS THE IDEAL FORM OF GOVERNMENT? HOW CAN MAN LEARN TO LIVE IN PEACE WITH HIS FELLOWS WITHOUT GIVING UP IMPORTANT AND NECESSARY FREEDOMS?"
HAURM?
I THOUGHT SO.
I THINK WE CAN BOTH AGREE THAT JUSTICE IS THE PRIMARY GOAL OF BOTH THE INDIVIDUAL AND THE STATE, BUT SINCE THE STATE IS BIGGER, ITS JUSTICE WILL BE LARGER AND EASIER TO STUDY...
...AND SINCE FOOD AND SHELTER IS THE PRIMARY NEED SUPPLIED BY THE STATE, THE STATE MUST CONSIST OF HUSBANDMAN, SHOEMAKER, WEAVER, BUILDER AND OTHERS, EACH SUPPLYING HIS GREATEST TALENT.
BUT THESE ALL NEED HERDSMAN, WEAVERS, CARPENTERS AND OTHERS TO SUPPORT THEM, AND THESE REQUIRE TRADERS, MERCHANTS, SAILORS, AGENTS AND BIG, BEEFY GUYS WHO CARRY THEM AROUND AND SCRAPE GLOP OFF YOUR SANDALS.
...ALL THESE PEOPLE MUST FIND JUSTICE AND THE JUSTICE WILL BE FOUND IN THE RELATIONS BETWEEN THEM, CORRECT? AND IS NOT THE FIRST INJUSTICE BROUGHT ON BY TYRANTS AND MERCENARIES? 'COURSE IT IS!
HAURRMMM...

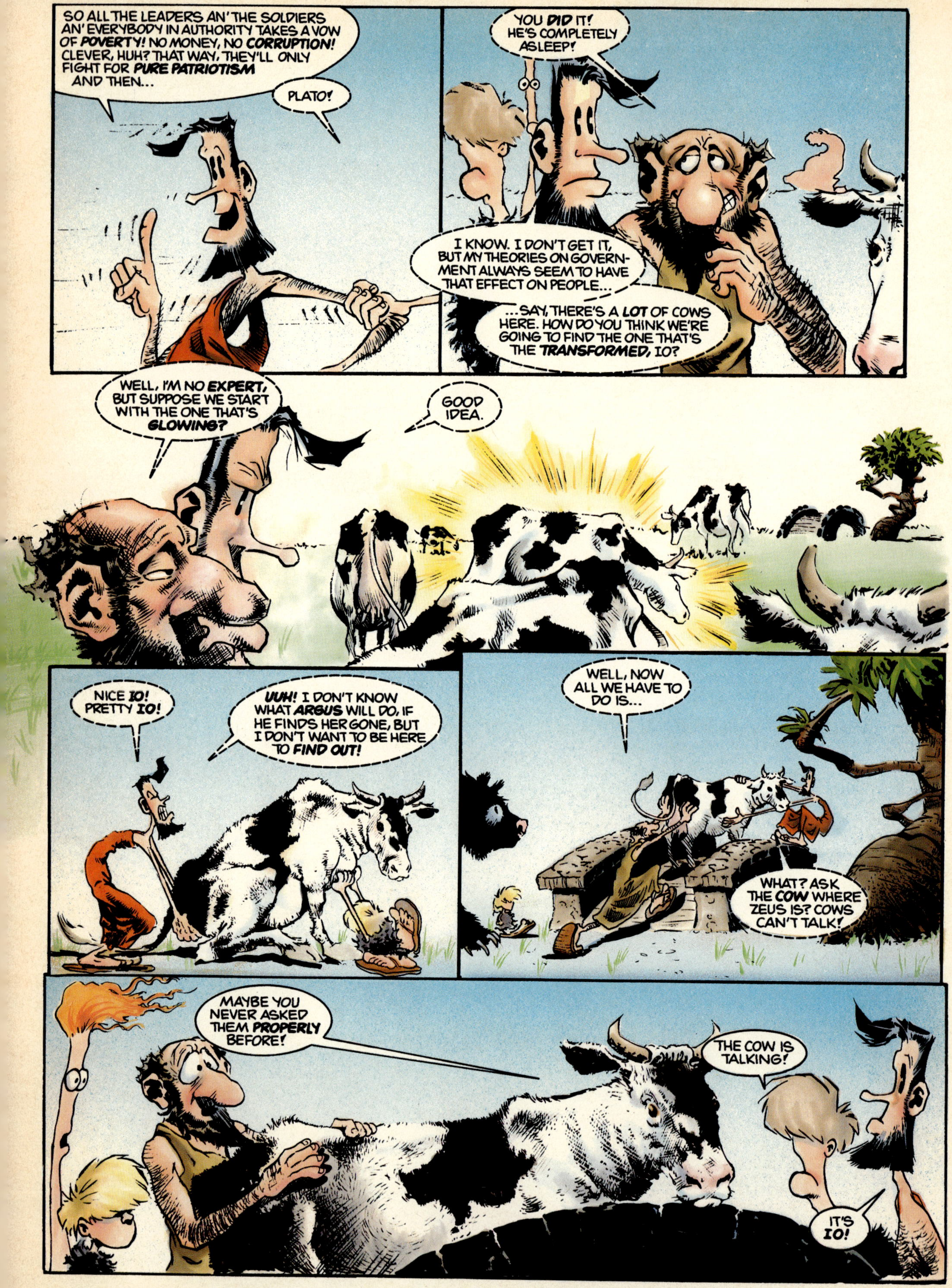

SO ALL THE LEADERS AN' THE SOLDIERS AN' EVERYBODY IN AUTHORITY TAKES A VOW OF POVERTY! NO MONEY, NO CORRUPTION! CLEVER, HUH? THAT WAY, THEY'LL ONLY FIGHT FOR PURE PATRIOTISM AND THEN...
PLATO!
YOU DID IT! HE'S COMPLETELY ASLEEP!
I KNOW. I DON'T GET IT, BUT MY THEORIES ON GOVERNMENT ALWAYS SEEM TO HAVE THAT EFFECT ON PEOPLE...
...SAY, THERE'S A LOT OF COWS HERE. HOW DO YOU THINK WE'RE GOING TO FIND THE ONE THAT'S THE TRANSFORMED, IO?
WELL, I'M NO EXPERT, BUT SUPPOSE WE START WITH THE ONE THAT'S GLOWING?
GOOD IDEA.
NICE IO! PRETTY IO!
UUH! I DON'T KNOW WHAT ARGUS WILL DO, IF HE FINDS HER GONE, BUT I DON'T WANT TO BE HERE TO FIND OUT!
WELL, NOW ALL WE HAVE TO DO IS...
WHAT? ASK THE COW WHERE ZEUS IS? COWS CAN'T TALK!
MAYBE YOU NEVER ASKED THEM PROPERLY BEFORE!
THE COW IS TALKING!
IT'S IO!

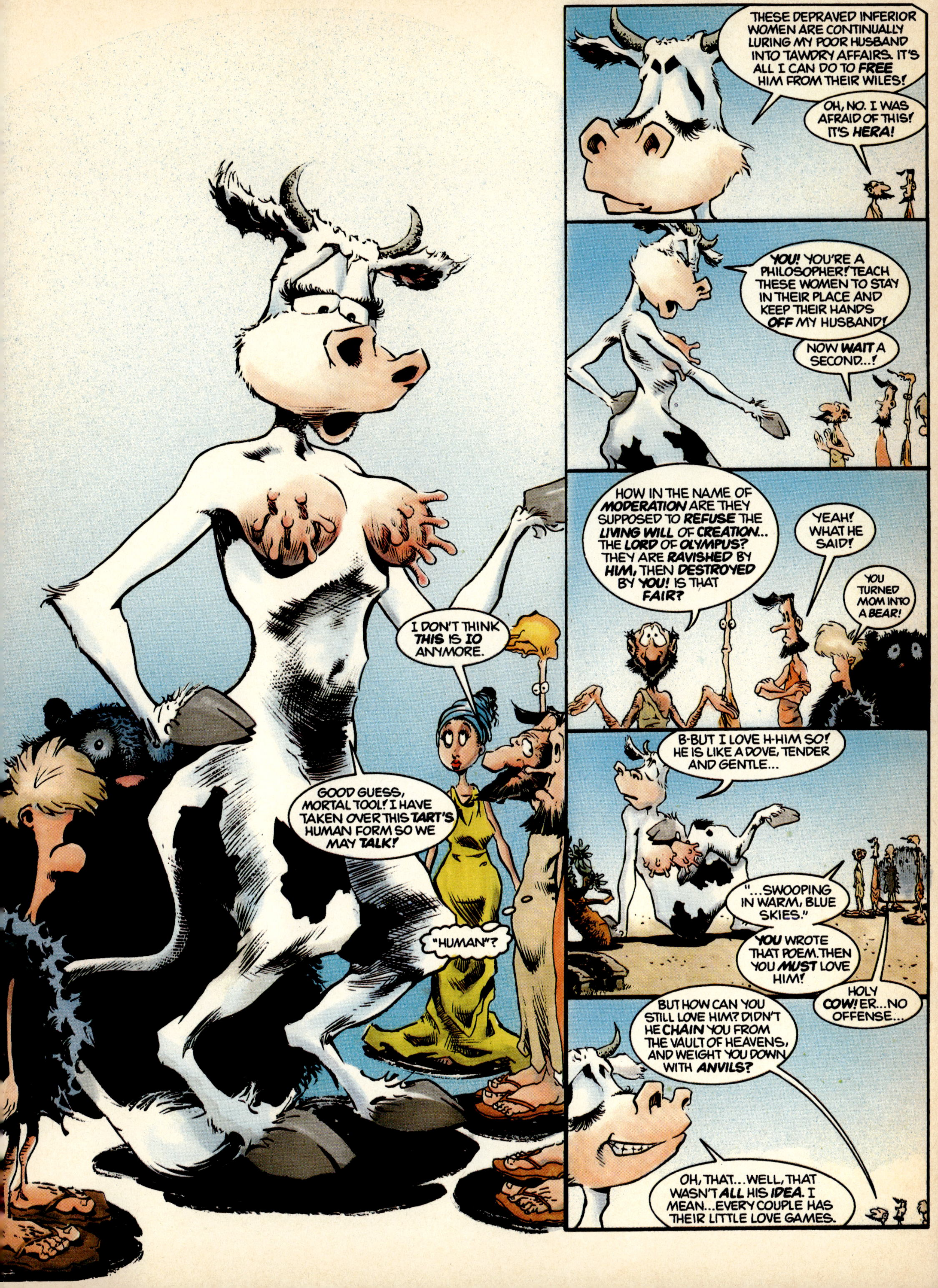
THESE DEPRAVED INFERIOR WOMEN ARE CONTINUALLY LURING MY POOR HUSBAND INTO TAWDRY AFFAIRS. IT'S ALL I CAN DO TO FREE HIM FROM THEIR WILES!
OH, NO. I WAS AFRAID OF THIS! IT'S HERA!
YOU! YOU'RE A PHILOSOPHER! TEACH THESE WOMEN TO STAY IN THEIR PLACE AND KEEP THEIR HANDS OFF MY HUSBAND!
NOW WAIT A SECOND...!
HOW IN THE NAME OF MODERATION ARE THEY SUPPOSED TO REFUSE THE LIVING WILL OF CREATION... THE LORD OF OLYMPUS? THEY ARE RAVISHED BY HIM, THEN DESTROYED BY YOU! IS THAT FAIR?
YEAH! WHAT HE SAID!
YOU TURNED MOM INTO A BEAR!
B-BUT I LOVE H-HIM SO! HE IS LIKE A DOVE, TENDER AND GENTLE...
"...SWOOPING IN WARM, BLUE SKIES."
YOU WROTE THAT POEM. THEN YOU MUST LOVE HIM!
HOLY COW! ER...NO OFFENSE...
BUT HOW CAN YOU STILL LOVE HIM? DIDN'T HE CHAIN YOU FROM THE VAULT OF HEAVENS, AND WEIGHT YOU DOWN WITH ANVILS?
OH, THAT... WELL, THAT WASN'T ALL HIS IDEA. I MEAN... EVERY COUPLE HAS THEIR LITTLE LOVE GAMES.
I DON'T THINK THIS IS IO ANYMORE.
GOOD GUESS, MORTAL TOOL! I HAVE TAKEN OVER THIS TART'S HUMAN FORM SO WE MAY TALK!
"HUMAN"?

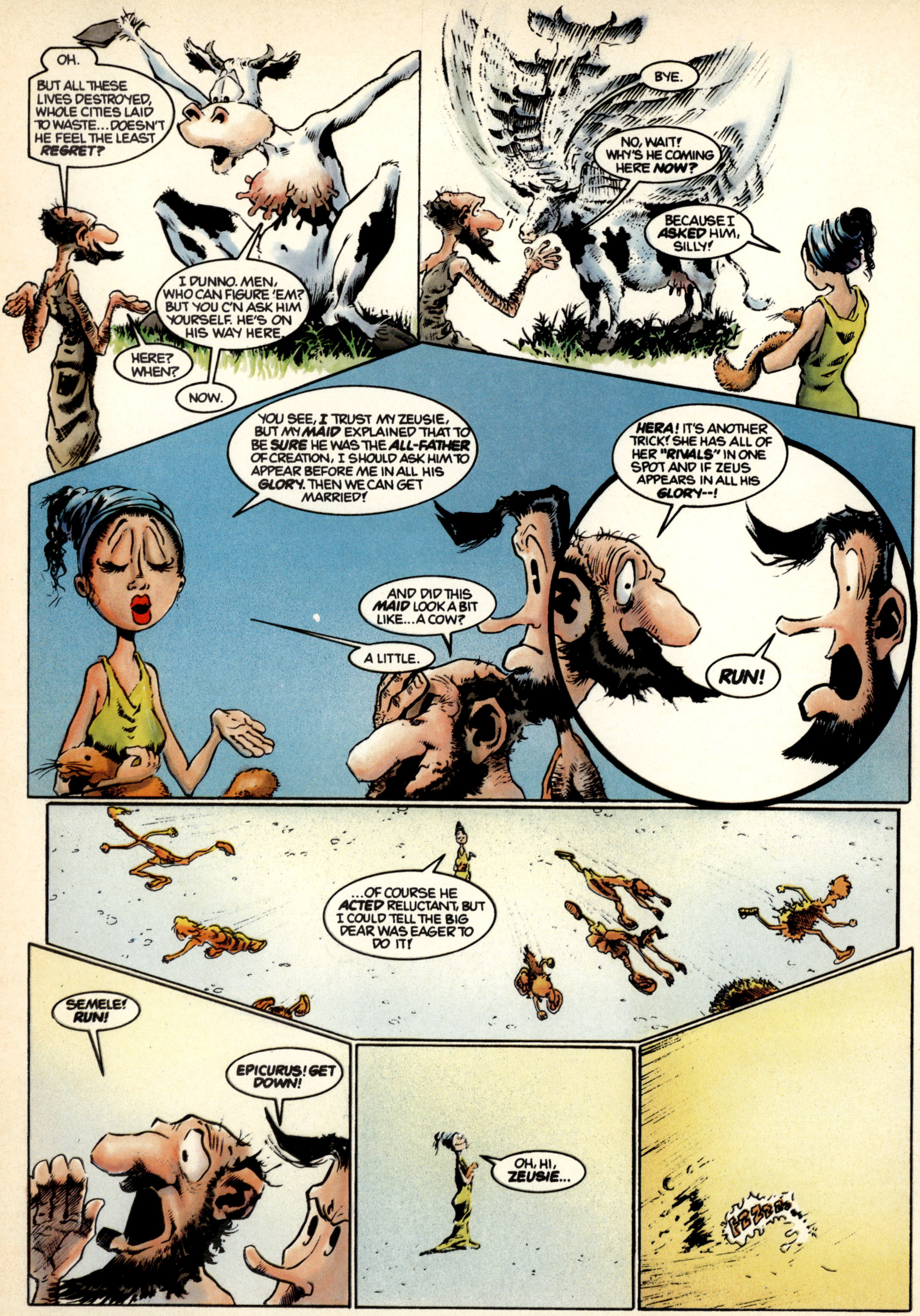
OH.
BUT ALL THESE LIVES DESTROYED, WHOLE CITIES LAID TO WASTE... DOESN'T HE FEEL THE LEAST REGRET?
I DUNNO. MEN, WHO CAN FIGURE 'EM? BUT YOU C'N ASK HIM YOURSELF. HE'S ON HIS WAY HERE.
HERE? WHEN?
NOW.
BYE.
NO, WAIT! WHY'S HE COMING HERE NOW?
BECAUSE I ASKED HIM, SILLY!
YOU SEE, I TRUST MY ZEUSIE, BUT MY MAID EXPLAINED THAT TO BE SURE HE WAS THE ALL-FATHER OF CREATION, I SHOULD ASK HIM TO APPEAR BEFORE ME IN ALL HIS GLORY. THEN WE CAN GET MARRIED!
AND DID THIS MAID LOOK A BIT LIKE... A COW?
A LITTLE.
HERA! IT'S ANOTHER TRICK! SHE HAS ALL OF HER "RIVALS" IN ONE SPOT AND IF ZEUS APPEARS IN ALL HIS GLORY--!
RUN!
...OF COURSE HE ACTED RELUCTANT, BUT I COULD TELL THE BIG DEAR WAS EAGER TO DO IT!
SEMELE! RUN!
EPICURUS! GET DOWN!
OH, HI, ZEUSIE...

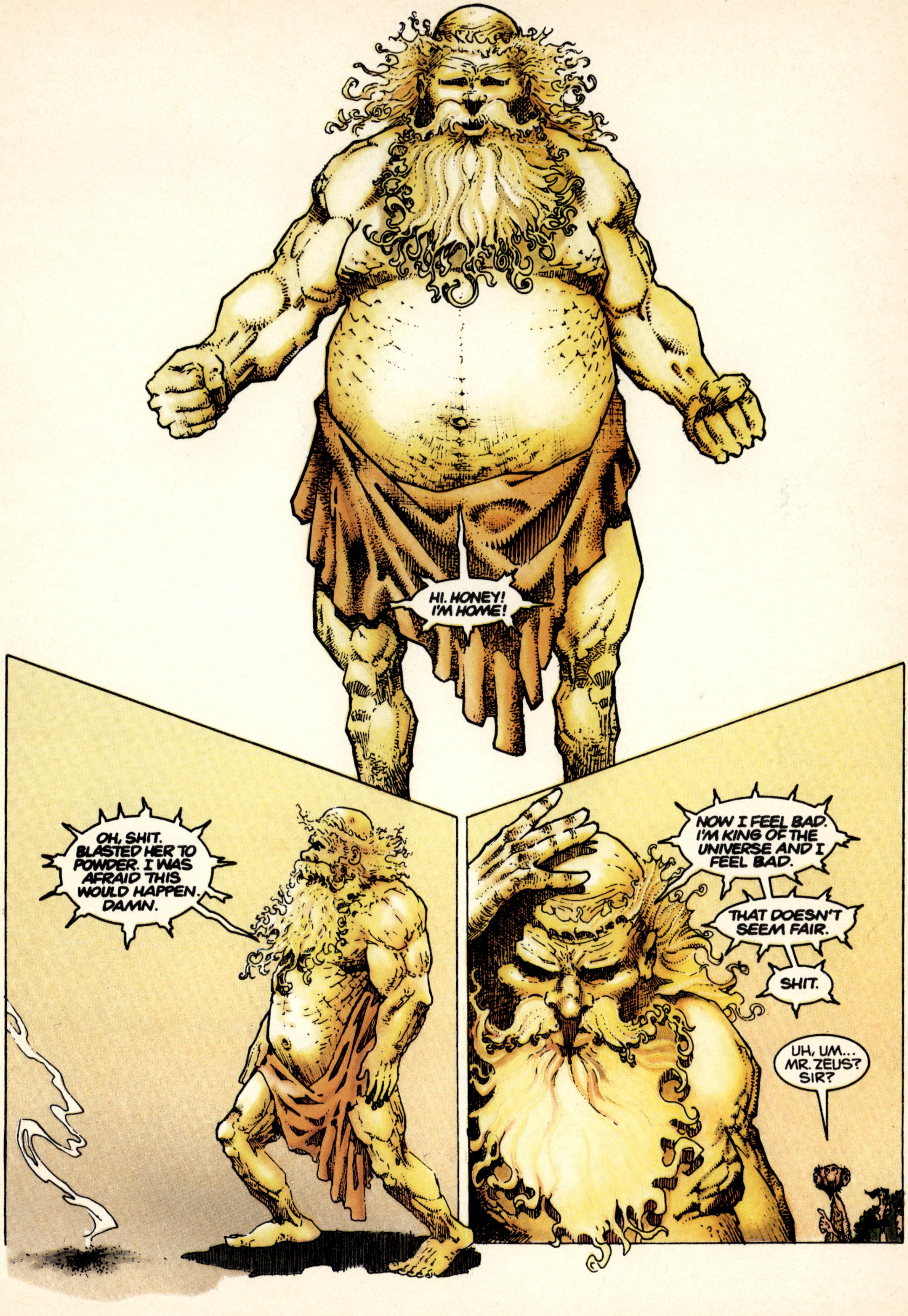
HI, HONEY! I'M HOME!
OH, SHIT. BLASTED HER TO POWDER. I WAS AFRAID THIS WOULD HAPPEN. DAMN.
NOW I FEEL BAD. I'M KING OF THE UNIVERSE AND I FEEL BAD.
THAT DOESN'T SEEM FAIR.
SHIT.
UH, UM... MR. ZEUS? SIR?

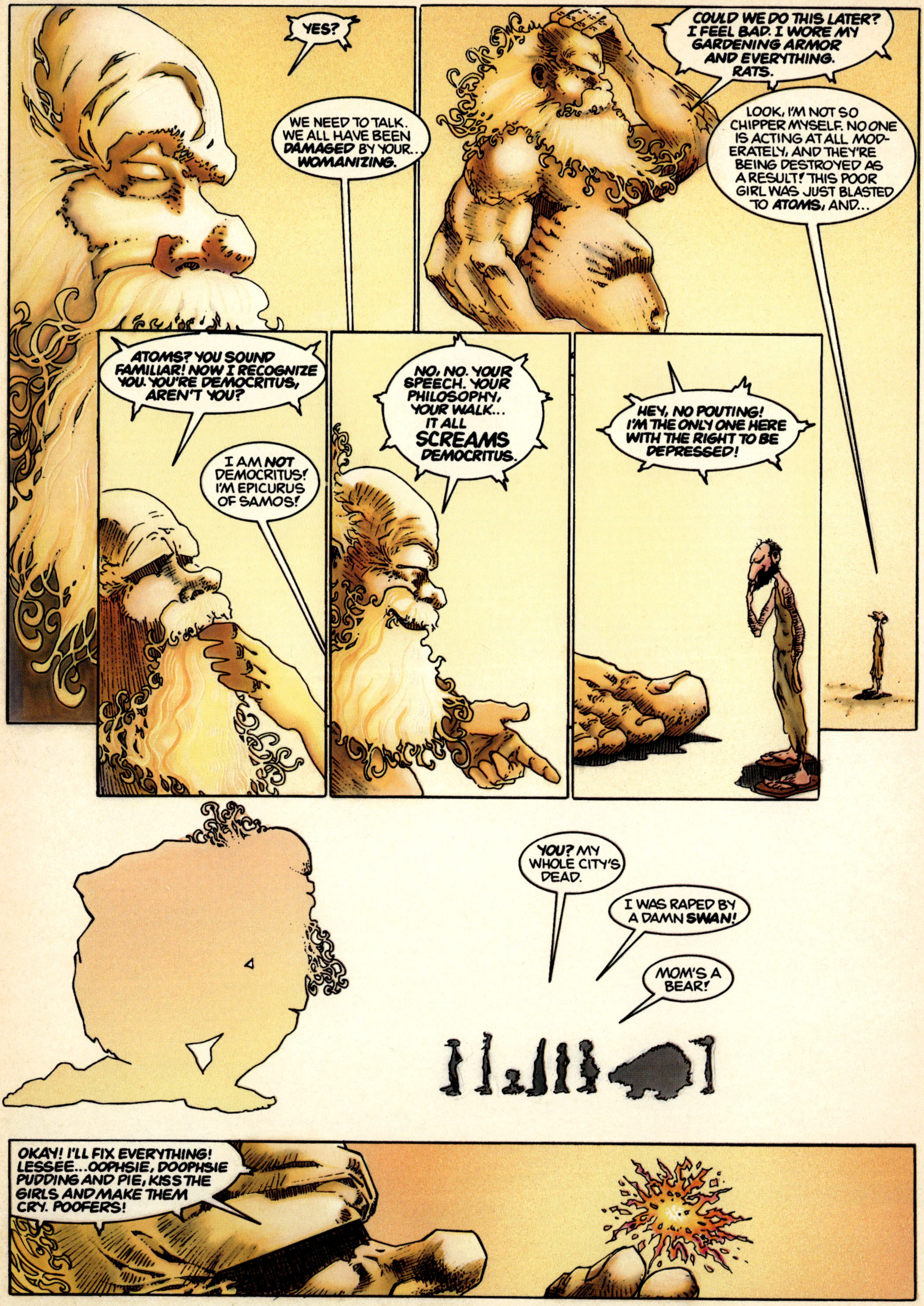
YES?
WE NEED TO TALK. WE ALL HAVE BEEN DAMAGED BY YOUR... WOMANIZING.
COULD WE DO THIS LATER? I FEEL BAD. I WORE MY GARDENING ARMOR AND EVERYTHING. RATS.
LOOK, I'M NOT SO CHIPPER MYSELF. NO ONE IS ACTING AT ALL MODERATELY, AND THEY'RE BEING DESTROYED AS A RESULT! THIS POOR GIRL WAS JUST BLASTED TO ATOMS, AND...
ATOMS? YOU SOUND FAMILIAR! NOW I RECOGNIZE YOU. YOU'RE DEMOCRITUS, AREN'T YOU?
I AM NOT DEMOCRITUS! I'M EPICURUS OF SAMOS!
NO, NO. YOUR SPEECH. YOUR PHILOSOPHY, YOUR WALK... IT ALL SCREAMS DEMOCRITUS.
HEY, NO POUTING! I'M THE ONLY ONE HERE WITH THE RIGHT TO BE DEPRESSED!
YOU? MY WHOLE CITY'S DEAD.
I WAS RAPED BY A DAMN SWAN!
MOM'S A BEAR!
OKAY! I'LL FIX EVERYTHING! LESSEE...OOPHSIE, DOOPHSIE PUDDING AND PIE, KISS THE GIRLS AND MAKE THEM CRY. POOFERS!

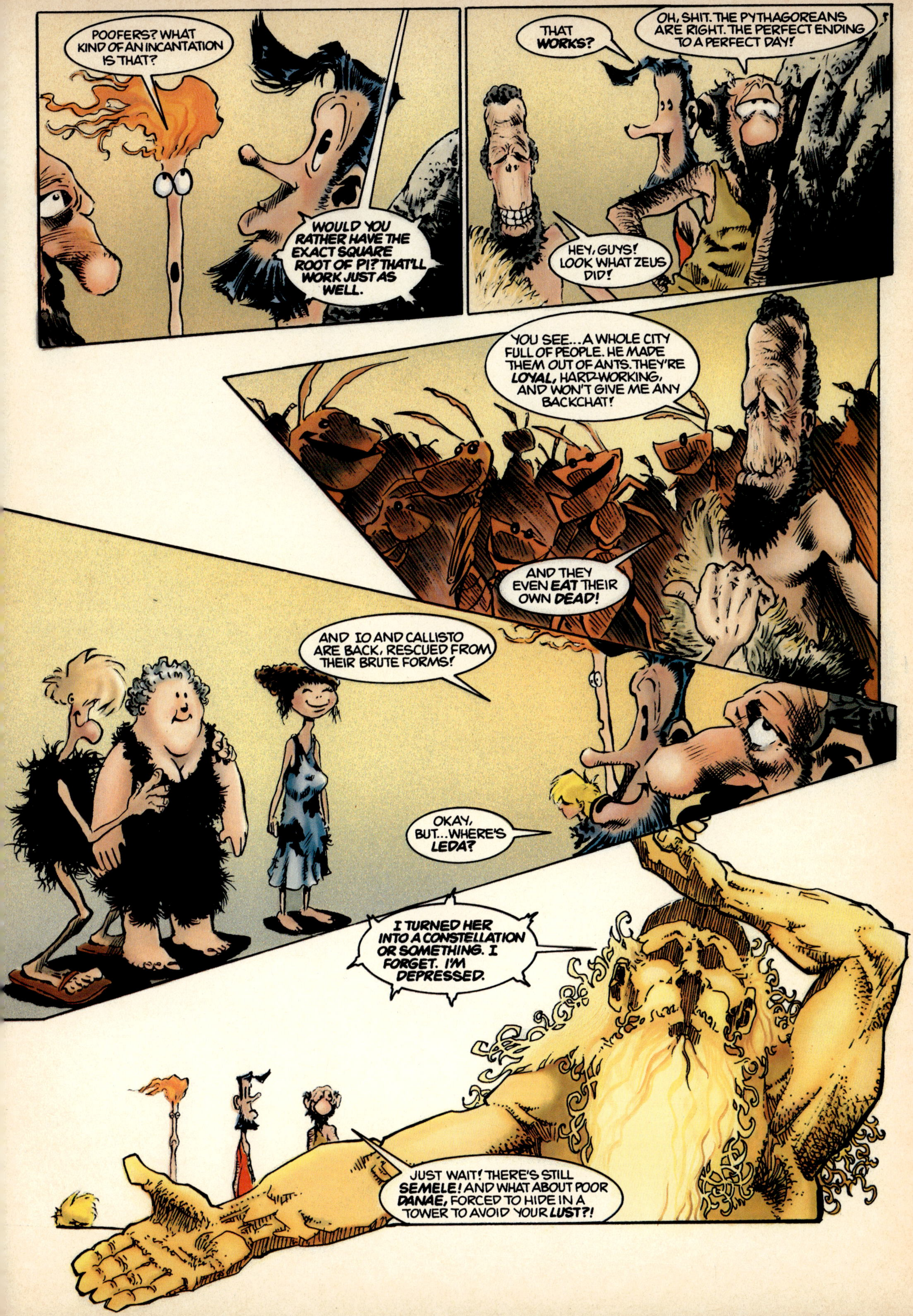
POOFERS? WHAT KIND OF AN INCANTATION IS THAT?
WOULD YOU RATHER HAVE THE EXACT SQUARE ROOT OF PI? THAT'LL WORK JUST AS WELL.
THAT WORKS?
OH, SHIT. THE PYTHAGOREANS ARE RIGHT. THE PERFECT ENDING TO A PERFECT DAY!
HEY, GUYS! LOOK WHAT ZEUS DID!
YOU SEE... A WHOLE CITY FULL OF PEOPLE. HE MADE THEM OUT OF ANTS. THEY'RE LOYAL, HARD-WORKING, AND WON'T GIVE ME ANY BACKCHAT!
AND THEY EVEN EAT THEIR OWN DEAD!
AND IO AND CALLISTO ARE BACK, RESCUED FROM THEIR BRUTE FORMS!
OKAY, BUT... WHERE'S LEDA?
I TURNED HER INTO A CONSTELLATION OR SOMETHING. I FORGET. I'M DEPRESSED.
JUST WAIT! THERE'S STILL SEMELE! AND WHAT ABOUT POOR DANAE, FORCED TO HIDE IN A TOWER TO AVOID YOUR LUST?!

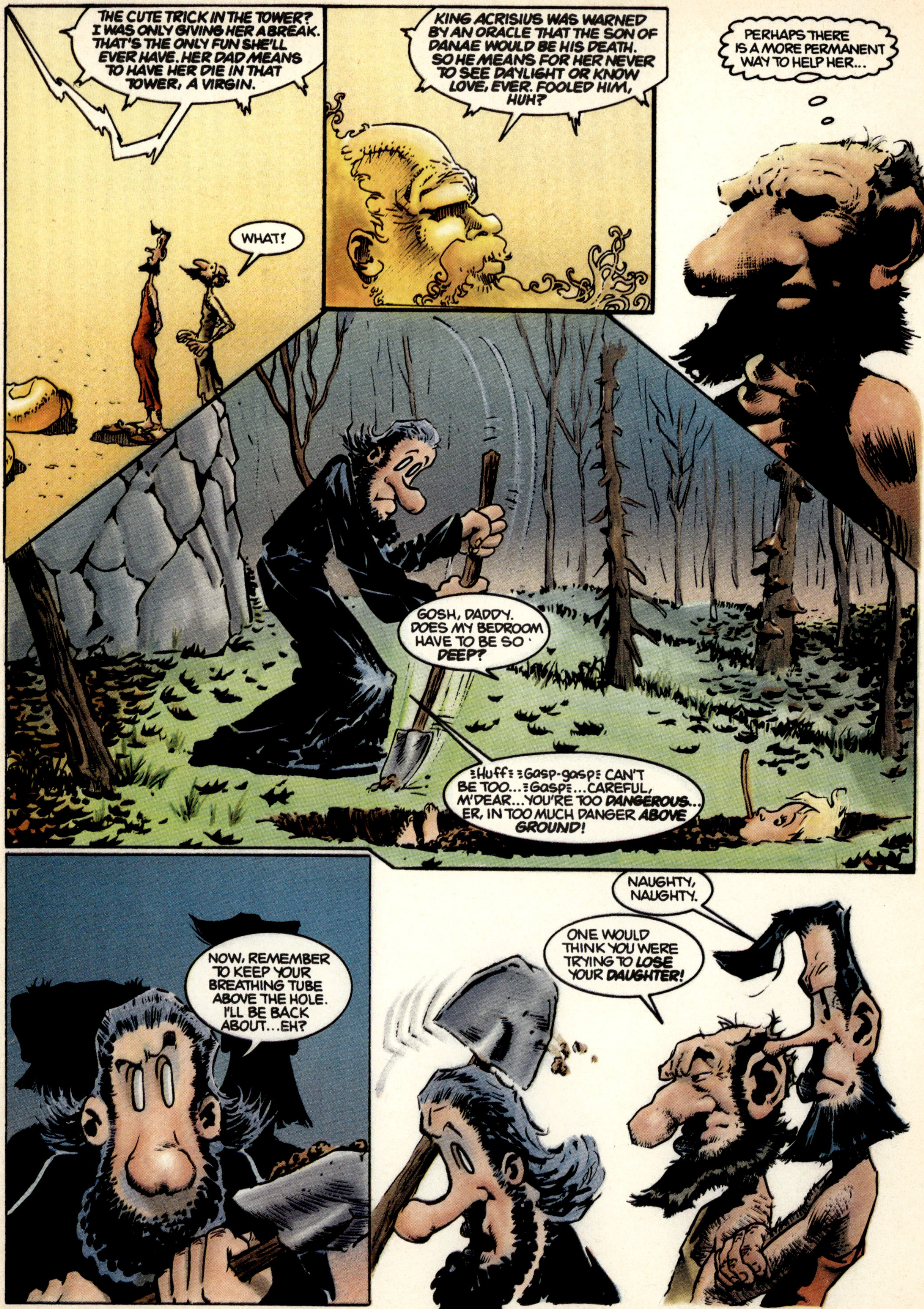
THE CUTE TRICK IN THE TOWER? I WAS ONLY GIVING HER A BREAK. THAT'S THE ONLY FUN SHE'LL EVER HAVE. HER DAD MEANS TO HAVE HER DIE IN THAT TOWER, A VIRGIN.
WHAT!
KING ACRISIUS WAS WARNED BY AN ORACLE THAT THE SON OF DANAE WOULD BE HIS DEATH. SO HE MEANS FOR HER NEVER TO SEE DAYLIGHT OR KNOW LOVE, EVER. FOOLED HIM, HUH?
PERHAPS THERE IS A MORE PERMANENT WAY TO HELP HER...
GOSH, DADDY. DOES MY BEDROOM HAVE TO BE SO DEEP?
:Huff: :Gasp-gasp: CAN'T BE TOO... :Gasp: ...CAREFUL, M'DEAR... YOU'RE TOO DANGEROUS... ER, IN TOO MUCH DANGER ABOVE GROUND!
NOW, REMEMBER TO KEEP YOUR BREATHING TUBE ABOVE THE HOLE. I'LL BE BACK ABOUT... EH?
NAUGHTY, NAUGHTY.
ONE WOULD THINK YOU WERE TRYING TO LOSE YOUR DAUGHTER!

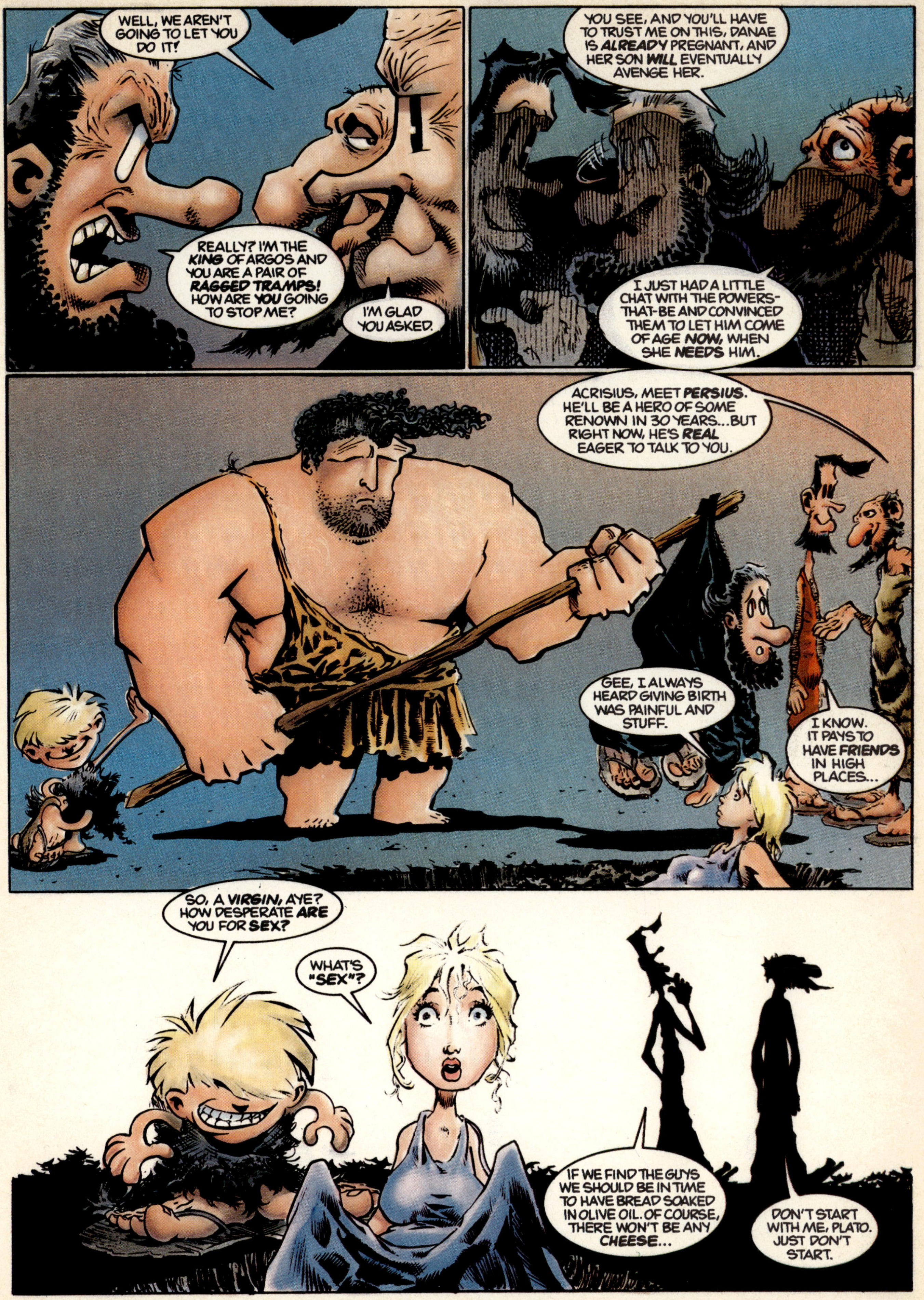

WELL, WE AREN'T GOING TO LET YOU DO IT!
REALLY? I'M THE KING OF ARGOS AND YOU ARE A PAIR OF RAGGED TRAMPS! HOW ARE YOU GOING TO STOP ME?
I'M GLAD YOU ASKED.
YOU SEE, AND YOU'LL HAVE TO TRUST ME ON THIS, DANAE IS ALREADY PREGNANT, AND HER SON WILL EVENTUALLY AVENGE HER.
I JUST HAD A LITTLE CHAT WITH THE POWERS-THAT-BE AND CONVINCED THEM TO LET HIM COME OF AGE NOW, WHEN SHE NEEDS HIM.
ACRISIUS, MEET PERSIUS. HE'LL BE A HERO OF SOME RENOWN IN 30 YEARS...BUT RIGHT NOW, HE'S REAL EAGER TO TALK TO YOU.
GEE, I ALWAYS HEARD GIVING BIRTH WAS PAINFUL AND STUFF.
I KNOW. IT PAYS TO HAVE FRIENDS IN HIGH PLACES...
SO, A VIRGIN, AYE? HOW DESPERATE ARE YOU FOR SEX?
WHAT'S "SEX"?
IF WE FIND THE GUYS WE SHOULD BE IN TIME TO HAVE BREAD SOAKED IN OLIVE OIL. OF COURSE, THERE WON'T BE ANY CHEESE...
DON'T START WITH ME, PLATO. JUST DON'T START.

PIRANHA PRESENTS

gregory

THE CELL IS SMALL

GREGORY IS SMALLER

He's a little guy with a big head, whose infectiously infantile behavior is restrained only by a size 3 straightjacket and four extra-firm concrete walls. He speaks mainly in vowels. Yes, Gregory is a lunatic — and quite happy about it, indeed!

And Gregory's world of abundant nothingness is chock full of sick humor, pathetic characters, and more neuroses than they've thought up names for. And, needless to say, it's loads of fun!

So, join Gregory and his rat friend Herman Vermin in their microcosmic loony-verse of pointless existence. After seeing the world in Gregory-vision, you just may consider babbling away inside a locked cell a viable option in life!

Ya know, it's guys like Gregory that give psychosis a good name...

Written and illustrated by Marc Hempel
120-page black-and-white trade paperback

Copyright © 1989 by Marc Hempel